The Budget Guide to Retail Store Planning & Design

REVISED 2ND EDITION

The Budget Guide to Retail Store Planning & Design

Jeff Grant

publications inc.

Cincinnati, Ohio

To adopt as a textbook or for permissions to reprint contact:

ST Publications Book Division
407 Gilbert Avenue
Cincinnati, Ohio 45202
U.S.A.

To contact the author write:

TRIO Display & Fixture Company, Inc.
5759 La Jolla Boulevard
La Jolla, California 92037
U.S.A.

Book design by Jeff Russ

Cover design by Paul Neff Design

Printed in the United States of America

ISBN 0-944094-10-4

CONTENTS

ABOUT THE AUTHOR

Jeff Grant's background in store design and planning covers three generations.

His grandfather, Victor, founded one of Los Angeles's earliest store fixture and display companies, Grant & Silvers, in 1931. The firm designed and built equipment and display props for many of the leading retail firms of that era. Grant & Silvers also manufactured the coconuts used in Hollywood's famous Coconut Grove nightclub.

Jeff's father, Marvin, worked with Victor until 1952. He then founded his own company to design stores and sell retail equipment. Marvin represented many store fixture manufacturers before he retired in 1988 and was named Salesman of the Year by the Western Association of Visual Merchandisers in 1983, the highest honor in the industry.

Jeff's initial chosen profession was law and he practiced as a business lawyer from 1976 through 1981. In October of 1981, Jeff learned that Jay Display, a San Diego display firm, was for sale. Jeff bought the company and orchestrated its growth into one of the largest store design and equipment firms in the Southwest. Jeff left the company in 1990 and established TRIO Display Group, a retail design and consulting firm in La Jolla, California.

Jeff is currently involved in the design and construction of many different types of stores in geographical areas ranging from Bangkok to Seattle. His specialty is gift, apparel and sports-related stores and his client list includes an extensive range of retail operations from mall stores to hospital gift shops. In addition, he has designed Team Shops for many professional sports teams including the Phoenix Suns, the L.A. Kings, the L.A. Clippers, the Cleveland Cavaliers, the Utah Jazz and Upper Deck Authenticated. Jeff lectures regularly at trade shows and has conducted seminars on store design and planning at the Impressions Show, the Hospital Gift Shop Show, the Super Show in Atlanta, the National Sporting Goods Show in Chicago and many more. In addition he has written articles on store planning for numerous publications.

Jeff can be reached in La Jolla. Phone: (619) 454-3134. FAX: (619) 454-3373.

FOREWORD

Over the past thirteen years I have been involved in the planning stages of many retail shops, and I have always been surprised at the lack of knowledge most prospective retailers exhibit regarding the process of creating or remodeling their stores. Most shop owners are ex-teachers, construction workers, students or homemakers and rarely come from a retail or business background. Many have no idea how to go about designing a "selling" environment, where to find a retail designer, what questions to ask concerning lay-out, colors, lighting, merchandising, or equipment, or even the budget required.

I decided to write this book after trying to find a simple guide to recommend to my retail clients, one they could buy at a reasonable price and that covered all the planning bases for a new store or a remodel. The books I did find on store planning were very expensive and were geared primarily toward large department or chain stores with open-ended budgets. My clients are primarily one to ten store operations owned by single entrepreneurs. They can't afford excessive design fees, high-end custom fixtures, or extensive construction build-outs. These retailers simply need an attractive store that sells merchandise.

This book addresses those merchants. I have attempted to provide enough information to plan a store either on your own or with the help of a retail designer. In addition, construction and equipment figures are furnished so you can create a reasonable and realistic budget. My goal is to show you how to create a fun, interesting store that sells merchandise. I hope this book can help you with that process.

Jeff Grant
October, 1994

INTRODUCTION

I have been involved in the design and construction of several hundred stores. All of the merchants have had different requirements that made their retailing and merchandising needs somewhat unique. Frankly, most of the shop owners I talk to about remodeling want to change the look of their stores for two reasons:

1) Pride of ownership: They want the store to reflect *their own image* of what a retail shop should look like. After all, this is their store and their ego and it is a lot more fun to have customers and competitors compliment the store than to hear disparaging remarks.

2) Increased sales: A well-designed shop will always increase sales, sometimes in amounts that are hard to believe. Although store layout is not the only factor in a retail shop's success, it is an important element in the overall struggle merchants of all sizes face in a competitive marketplace. Increasingly, the store design element has become a major concern to the farsighted retailer.

Of course, having an attractive, well-merchandised store is an important element in any profitable retail operation. However, design alone will not ensure success. My experience as a lawyer, designer, contractor and equipment supplier has put me in contact with thousands of retailers both large and small. Certain principles seem to ensure success while others guarantee failure. The maxims that I consistently see applied

to all retailers run something like this:

1) Location: If you have the right one, it is hard go wrong. With a good location, you can have the worst merchandise with the highest prices and the surliest help and you will still sell goods. Why? Because a great location is either:

a) In a high-traffic spot where people are in a buying mood, such as a mall or a theme center.

b) In a remote location where the retailer may be the only game in town or close to it, such as a hotel, resort or small town.

c) In a busy strip center or a well-traveled shopping street.

2) A well-negotiated lease: If your rent is too high, your sales will never cover the overhead. Negotiate rent, tenant improvements, cost of living increases, available uses and every other clause that has a bearing on your ability to make a go of the store.

3) Personnel: Unfriendly, uninformed or unprofessional salespeople can kill your business. Period. Make sure your people are well-trained in both the retail sales trade and the personality game. How many of us hire young part-time help only to see sales and profits dive while shrinkage seems to rise? If you are careful about whom you pick to work in the shop, train consistently about product and salesmanship, and provide incentives for productivity, your sales and profits will soar along with shop morale.

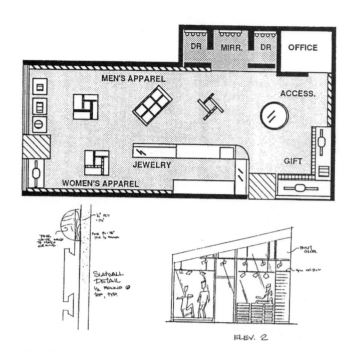

A well-planned store will always sell more than a store that's just thrown together.

4) Pricing: Too low and you can't pay the bills. Too high, and the best location, people and store design won't compensate. Shop your competition and don't become complacent.

5) Advertising: If people don't know you exist, they won't come to shop. If you think you're busy now due to your great location, how much busier would you be if more people knew where you were and what you offered? Be aggressive about your marketing. You are not there just to have fun.

6) Store Design: An interesting, well-planned store will always sell more goods than one where merchandise is thrown about with little rhyme or reason. Pull customers into the store with effective windows and signage. Lure them through every aisle with effective merchandising and lighting. Whet their buying appetite with dynamic displays and finish off the sale with competitive prices and professional salesmanship.

Any of the above elements alone will not guarantee a retailer's success. However, by combining them effectively, a shop's chances of succeeding profitably are all but ensured. I can't tell you whom to hire or how to price your goods, but I can tell you how to build a store that customers will want to shop in. A store that creates a buying atmosphere. A store that the owner will be proud of. In fact, a store that is designed to sell merchandise and make money. Perhaps most importantly, a store that won't cost a fortune to build.

I don't know if you are buying your merchandise correctly or picking the correct products. That's for other consultants to address. But if you're not sure how to handle those aspects of your retail operations, get help. You can only learn about retail by "doing it" or by talking to people who have. You are making a significant investment in time and money. Do it right.

This book has been laid out in the order most retailers follow in the process of initiating a new store or remodeling an existing space. I do not discuss the financial aspects of the decision-making process except as it applies to the costs incurred in leasing, design, construction and equipment.

I suggest you leaf through this book before you dig in to any particular section. Get a feel for how it applies to your particular needs. Maybe at this point you just need some help with lighting or floor coverings. Fine, keep the book for later analysis.

One recommendation I will make. Don't get complacent with your store. Go through this and other design books every few months just to jog your idea bank. Look at other shops of all kinds, regularly noting both the merchandise and the displays. Finally, make your store a fun place to visit and pass that attitude along to your employees. Your shop should be a place where regular customers come in all the time just to see "what's new." In other words, try to make your shop your customers' "favorite store."

1

1 BUDGETING STORE DESIGN, CONSTRUCTION AND EQUIPMENT

The first step in any retail store's creation is a "realistic" budget evaluation of everything that will be required to lease, design, build, equip, stock and open the new facility. Without a budget, the merchant won't know how much stock she will be carrying, what her operating expenses will be, how much merchandise she will need to sell, and most importantly in the early design stages, how much money will be available for building the store.

Many clients come to my firm with absolutely no idea of the costs involved in opening a new store or in remodeling an old one. In some cases, a budget has been established for the store's opening that is unrealistic in light of the image or concept the prospective merchant intends to convey.

Further, many fledgling retailers, fresh from the negotiating school that espouses, "get the other guy's price first," are convinced that if they disclose their true construction budget to the person designing their store, he will spend every last penny of it. Unfortunately, the result of this lack of communication is a store that either costs well in excess of the retailer's ability to pay, or a cheap store that in no way reflects the look the retailer was after. In either event, the result is both disappointing and a waste of design fees that will now need to be spent again.

Once you've made up your mind that you want to be in retail and you have figured out just what it is that

you want to sell, put together an income/expense projection with your accountant to check the long-term viability of the project. If those numbers are optimistic, add up the required startup costs involved so you know just how much money you will need for your initial capital investment and how much will be available to design, supply and build the store.

The fixed initial expenses will include:
• Business and resale licenses
• Lease deposits and initial rents
• Legal fees and insurance
• Phone and utility hook-ups

To figure out your merchandise requirements, compute:
• The amount of money you need to cover fixed and variable expenses
• The actual cost of your goods
• The quantity of inventory and number of inventory turns you will need to do in a year to make a living and show a profit

What about working capital? It may take a some time to become profitable, so set some money aside to pay the bills while you're operating in the red.

Take the initial expenses, your merchandise requirements and required working capital, and subtract it from your retail nest egg. The sum left is what you have available to build the store. Whether or not it is enough is really a question of just what you want your

Typical budget requirements for a 2000-square-foot clothing or gift shop in a mall

Permits	This will vary from town to town and is usually a percentage of the total construction cost.	$200-2000
Storefront	20´ wide x 8´ high front with large display windows and door will cost approx. $2640.00.	$16.50 per sq. ft.
Walls	Includes dressing room and storage area walls.	$23.00 per ft.
Standard Bath	This includes handicapped requirements.	$4500.00
Ceiling	Varies based on tile used. 2´ x 4´ tiles are the least expensive.	$1-2.50 per ft.
Lighting	Fluorescent lighting with some incandescent track lamps.	$4-5.50 per sq. ft.
Receptacles	Duplex outlets for electrical.	$40.00 ea.
Floorings	Prices vary based on type of carpet and resilient flooring.	$1-10 per sq. ft.
Paint	Very wide variance in price. Contractor's price is per coat.	$0.30 per sq. ft.
HVAC	Heating and air conditioning.	$5-6 per sq. ft.
Store Fixtures	Varies based on the look and sophistication of the store.	$5-25 per sq. ft.
Front Signage	Depends on type of sign used: neon, channel letters, box, etc.	$750-5000

The bottom line: Mall stores under 3000 sq. ft. seem to average $40 to $75 per sq. ft. Strip center stores with bathrooms, HVAC, ceilings, and lighting provided run $10-25 per sq. ft.

Note: These figures are based on current pricing for construction in San Diego, California, at time of publication.

store to look like. If you add up all your expenses and determine that you only have $5,000 to 7,000 left to build out and purchase fixtures for your new 2000-square-foot store, then you might need to rethink your merchandise requirements or your initial investment. (Or find a lot of used store equipment.)

Throughout this book, I will give you some ideas of costs for specific projects. However, as an initial guideline, refer to the chart at the top of the page.

Keep in mind that the least malleable figures are those charged by construction people. You will find on a very consistent basis that licensed subcontractors in every trade charge substantially the same prices. The only way to save money on the construction end is to do the work yourself. (See the chapter on construction.) The flooring, lighting, fixtures and signage will all have a variable price based upon the level of sophistication and complexity of your store.

Don't rely on ballpark figures. Set a realistic budget, disclose it to your designer, contractor and fixture supplier, and give them time to design and bid the job correctly. That is the only way you will ever build the store you want at a price you can afford.

Several years ago I was approached by a retailer from New York who had leased space in La Jolla, California. He asked me if I could build him a 1200-square-foot store for $25,000 or less and could I do so within 30 days. I asked him if he had a copy of the plans and he informed me they had not yet been drafted. I looked at the space and told him that certain walls he wanted removed might contain structural components that would have to be dealt with. Further, until a complete store plan had been drafted and we had done some preliminary research, I couldn't commit on price.

The retailer found a contractor who would commit without plans or research at a ballpark figure of $23,000 to $27,000. The project was started without a plan, structural problems were encountered, the city held up permits waiting on engineering drawings, the fixtures and equipment had to be downgraded to s upport the extended construction budget, etc. The store eventually came in at over $40,000, opened late, and did not look nearly as nice as the merchant had envisioned it would.

One final note on budgeting. Make sure your designer gives you variables for each design element that will adjust the budget. For instance:

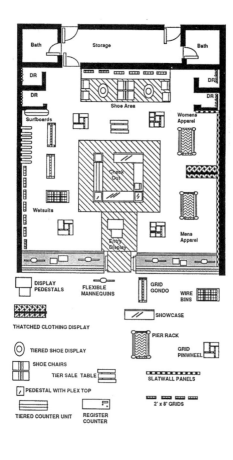

Schedule A
Smith Surf Shop

Framing
  1. Full height partitions 3 5/20, 16oc, 5/8 x 2 x 18   110
  2. Interior partitions 3 5/25, 16oc, 5/8 x 2 x 10   63
  3. Doors 3 /0 x 6/8 Timely, Legacy per plan
  4. Marlite standard 1/8″ w/reg. trim 288 sq. ft.
  5. Restroom Finish   a. T.P. roll
                       b. Grabbars
                       c: Paper towel
                       d. M/W signs $ 6,270.00

Electric Furnish and install electrical wiring in accordance with National Electrical Code, local codes and plans including the following:
  28 - 2″ x 4″ 4-tube fluorescent lighting fixtures
  3 - exit lighting fixtures
  2 - power to bath fans
  12 - duplex receptacles
  11 - single-pole switches
  8 - 3-way switches
  2 - 4-way switches
  6′ of plugmold with 12 receptacles in storage assume 50 amp 208 volt 30 power to A/C disconnect on roof.
  Processing of plans at City of San Diego including Title 24 calculations.
  Installation of indicated power track for track lighting.
  Installation of dressing room lamps.
  Excluded: temporary power, power company charges. $ 6,075.00

HVAC Installation of 1 4-ton packaged heat pump roof top unit. Bid includes all parts and labor. Except: electric to unit by others and drain lines by others. Bid also includes 2 bath exhaust fans, Title 24 calculations and preparing mechanical sheet for HVAC for permit. $ 5,000.00

Paint All interior walls existing and new. One coat of primer, one coat finish color per plan. $ 2,500.00

Mirror 1 mirror each bath and dressing room $ 700.00

Ceiling New ceiling per plan $ 5,000.00

Permits Estimated cost $ 250.00

Installation of grids, slatwall, and all loose fixtures per plan $ 4,500.00

Supervision $ 3,750.00
Subtotal $34,045.00
Profit and overhead (20%) $ 6,809.00
Total $40,854.00

These pages show a typical preliminary budget review for a 2400-square-foot specialty shop. Pricing includes the landlord's share so a true dollar figure can be ascertained.

• A nylon carpet will cost $14 to $30 per yard while an Olefin/nylon blend will only run $8 to $12 per yard. A 2000-square-foot store requires about 220 yards.

• A curved front counter may cost twice as much as one that is square with angled ends.

• Used, refinished mannequins are one-half the price of new ones.

• A standard white or gray slatwall costs 33% less than a custom-colored, high-pressure laminate.

• Imported track lights may run 20% less than a domestic brand. The bulbs provide the correct light, not the lighting fixture, so save your money.

• A demising wall that extends all the way to the ceiling may require lights, sprinkler heads and air conditioning ducts to be moved, while a wall that stops within 18 inches of the ceiling will not require any relocation of existing equipment.

I could go on. However, all you need to remember is that there are many ways to cut costs without sacrificing quality or style. You simply need to ask. Just make sure you ask not only your designer, but your contractor, your fixture supplier and your floor-covering dealer this simple question, "Where can we cut costs and what effect will it have on the look of the store and its ability to sell merchandise?" Then you can make an informed decision regarding the equipment and design elements you will incorporate into your store.

DESIGNHOUSE
COMMERCIAL AND RETAIL DESIGN

Joe Smith
Joe's Surf Shop
4728 Fifth. St. Suite B
San Diego, CA

Dear Joe,
The following represents our estimate of the costs required for the design, construction and fixtures for your new store. We are basing these figures on the preliminary design enclosed and the numbers may change somewhat once we fine tune the project.

Design
Our "upset" design figure is $5000.00 and I think we will stay under that. That number includes concept as well as working drawings and allows for some job supervision.

Construction
The preliminary construction bid is attached as exhibit A. Most of these costs will be covered by the Landlord's tenant improvement allowance so you should talk to him about those expenses ASAP. Total overall cost is $40,854.00. Building costs are pretty fixed so I don't think we have much flexibility here.

Floorcoverings
We are going to go with a combination of wood plank at the entry, rubber tiles in the windows, vinyl sheet in the backrooms and carpet everywhere else. Carpet will be a Harbinger 42 oz. nylon. Costs will be as follows.

1 lot	Floor prep	$250.00	$ 250.00
300 ft.	Wood plank	$ 6.00	$1800.00
300 ft.	Vinyl Sheet	$ 2.00	$ 600.00
200 yds.	Harbinger carpet	$ 29.00	$5800.00
375 ft.	4″ top set base	$ 1.50	$ 562.50
70 ft.	Rubber tile	$ 6.00	$ 420.00
Total flooring			$9432.00

We can save money in this area by using a different carpet and switching the wood from plank to either vinyl wood strips or wood tiles.

Lighting
We are recommending 90 watt spot lights mounted on track to supplement the fluorescent fixtures. These will be needed in the windows and in numerous places throughout the store to create focal points in your merchandising scheme. We are specifying an inexpensive light can and a Sylvania Capsylite bulb.

180 ft.	track	$ 5.00	$ 900.00
40	cylinder style light cans with bulbs	$35.00	$1400.00
Total Lighting			$2300.00

Fixtures
These are the prices for the fixtures you and I came up with. This combination of custom and off-the-shelf equipment should keep the budget in line with our earlier projections.

13	2′ x 8′ white grids	$ 35.00	$ 455.00
52	grid wall brackets	$ 3.00	$ 156.00
2	grid gondolas with bases	$ 250.00	$ 500.00
4	grid pinwheels with bases	$ 300.00	$ 1200.00
1 lot	grid display allowance	$1000.00	$ 1000.00
2	pier racks	$ 350.00	$ 700.00
1	wire bin unit	$ 185.00	$ 185.00
1	sale tier table	$ 525.00	$ 525.00
2	round tier shoe display	$ 350.00	$ 700.00
4	window pedestal displays	$ 75.00	$ 150.00
4	tube forms	$ 150.00	$ 150.00
1 lot	allowance for signage and display	$2000.00	$ 2000.00
1 lot	counters and cases	$3200.00	$ 3200.00
10	4′ x 8′ slatwall panels with inserts	$ 75.00	$ 750.00
Total fixtures			$11,571.00

Summary

Total Design	$ 5,000.00	
Total Construction	$40,854.00	
Total Flooring	$ 9,432.00	
Total Lighting	$ 2,300.00	
Total Fixtures	$11,571.00	
Subtotal		$66,880.00
Less landlord reimbursement		$35,000.00
Total		$31,880.00

Look this over and give me a call. If we need to cut, now is the time to do so.
Thanks.

2

2 RETAIL LEASE ANALYSIS AND NEGOTIATION

A prerequisite to success in most retail endeavors is the existence of a reasonable lease that doesn't bury the tenant in rent, percentage payments, common area and advertising fees, and restrictive use provisions. The rest of your operation can be perfectly organized but if the margins and sales volume obtainable at that location can't support the rent, you will fail.

As a consultant and attorney I've had the opportunity to review and negotiate many retail leases from the tenant's point of view. Based on that experience I can state with confidence, *"Store leases are never fair."* At least not as far as the tenant is concerned. Most tenants just sign the lease placed in front of them with a minimum amount of negotiation. In fact, with a few murmured assurances about standard provisions and boilerplate clauses, many commercial leases are simply glanced at and signed. Tenant improvement allowances, triple net and common area charges, CPI adjustments, subleasing and other negotiable clauses are either not discussed or are glossed over.

Your lease agreement can make or break your business. It should be reviewed and analyzed with that supposition in mind. The following is a list of items that must be carefully addressed in every retail lease negotiation. The list does not cover every aspect of every lease nor does it purport to do so. However, this list will give you a headstart in negotiating a

better deal, minimizing risks and understanding what the "real cost" of the lease will be.

Most standard leases contain approximately 30 standard provisions and the difference between a fair and unfair lease from the tenant's point of view might hinge on several well-turned phrases. If your level of sophistication lies elsewhere, work with an accomplished commercial broker or invest in a good lawyer who can analyze the provisions you are or should be uncomfortable with. A little negotiation before you sign the lease can save you thousands of dollars over its term.

Remember a few things about negotiating a lease:

1) The more chips on the table, the easier it is to get some of them in your pocket. Negotiate each lease clause that is important to you. These will probably include:
a) Rent and increases
b) Use clauses
c) Tenant improvement allowances
d) Term of lease and options
e) Assignments and subleasing
f) Start dates
g) Common area and advertising fees

2) Go ahead and ask for what you want. The worst the landlord can do is say no.

3) Every penny that gets saved per foot in rent gets multiplied by the term of the lease. A 5¢ per foot savings in a 2500-square-foot space over a 5-year term will save you $7500.

4) The tighter the rental market, the harder it is to negotiate. A well-located property with few vacancies translates in to a hardnosed landlord. On the other hand, a soft market or a building that has vacancy problems will provide a ripe opportunity to negotiate many lease concessions in your favor.

5) Keep in mind that location is everything and a long-vacant center may mean the location is not one you want to consider renting.

6) Research the market and try to have several other lease proposals in hand before you sit down to negotiate with your landlord.

7) Don't negotiate the lease to death. If you are satisfied with the location and need to proceed with your store planning and construction, compromise. Try to work out a deal with the landlord that is "close enough" to what you want. If you're simply too far apart, drop the deal and move on.

Again, try not to negotiate the lease on your own. Use an experienced real estate broker or lawyer who represents only you. Many brokers and lawyers have not dealt with retail leases, so try to find someone with experience in this area. A typical fee for a lease negotiation and analysis is $450 to 1000 and it's worth every penny. Not only do experienced real estate brokers and lawyers know what to look for in the lease and what can be negotiated in the market-place, but they can also act as a buffer between you and the other parties. Sometimes emotion and subjectivity can get in the way of objective business decisions. A professional can retain objectivity while leading all parties involved toward a satisfactory lease negotiation and a signed contract.

Finally take the time to read and understand your lease. It's something you'll have to live with for quite a few years and may in fact turn out to be the most important document in your business portfolio.

Negotiate your lease!

The effects of negotiating even a few cents per foot off of a long term lease can be quite dramatic as the following chart demonstrates:

Assume a 2,000 sq. ft. space in a retail strip center:

Lease Amount	$1.25 sq. ft.	$1.30 sq. ft.	$1.35 sq. ft.	$1.50 sq. ft.
Lease Term		Total Rents Paid		
3 year	$9,000	$9,350	$9,720	$10,800
5 year	$15,000	$15,6000	$16,200	$18,000
7 year	$21,000	$21,840	$22,680	$25,200

Then plug in the effect of Cost-of-Living increases based on a percentage of your total rent which is then compounded annually by the previous increases. A few pennies per month can save thousands of dollars over the long term.

RETAIL LEASE CHECKLIST

The following is a list of standard lease clauses that should be analyzed prior to signing any lease. This list is not fully complete and any lease that you contemplate signing should be carefully examined by your real estate broker and lawyer.

A. Date and Parties
1. Is the lease correctly dated?
2. Are the landlord and lessee accurately described with full legal names, correct states of incorporation, and principal business addresses?
3. Have the correct parties, partners or corporate officers signed the lease?

B. Premises
Make sure you get exactly what you rented. Carefully measure your space and compare the space actually being used with the space listed in the lease.
1. Are the The Premises fully and accurately described?
2. Are exhibits referred to and attached showing the legal description and the location and floor plan of The Premises and building?
3. Is the square footage of The Premises specifically stated?
4. Is the square footage measured by rentable square feet including portions of common areas, or by usable square feet limited to space within the four walls of The Premises, or by some other method?

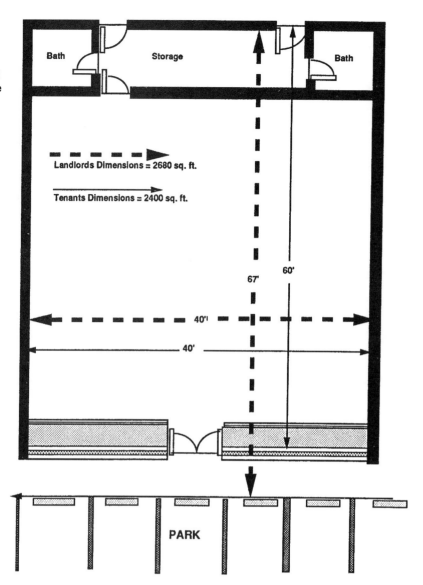

Make sure you and the landlord are measuring your space in the same manner.

Bath   Storage   Bath

Landlords Dimensions = 2680 sq. ft.

Tenants Dimensions = 2400 sq. ft.

67'   60'

40'

40'

PARK

5. If the The Premises cannot be measured because the building is still under construction, how will it be measured and how will size discrepancies be treated?
6. Are specific parking places provided for?
7. What if the parking spaces are unavailable due to new construction on the shopping center?

C. Term
1. Are the commencement and termination dates specific?
2. If the commencement date is not specific because the building is under construction, will the Tenant receive adequate advance written notice when The Premises will be ready?
3. What triggers Tenant's obligation to move in and pay rent? Substantial completion? Is substantial completion defined, for example, as when the Tenant is able to use The Premises for their intended purposes, or when the certificate of occupancy is issued, or by the time the premises are ready per specifications?
4. What if the Tenant's interior spaces are complete, but the exterior of the building is still in the finish stages surrounded by scaffolding or other construction materials?

5. How is a dispute decided over whether The Premises are ready? By negotiation; by mediation; by arbitration; by Landlord's reasonable judgment; by Landlord's architect; or by an architect chosen by both parties?

D. Delayed Possession
1. If possession is delayed through no fault of Tenant, what remedies does Tenant have? Rent abatement; money damages; cancellation; or reimbursement for prepaid monies, such as the security deposit and the first month's rent; or all of these remedies?
2. Are the commencement and termination dates extended in a time period equal to any delay?

E. Rent
1. Is the agreed-upon rental amount specifically stated?
2. If the rent is stated in more than one way (monthly, annually, per square foot, for a full term), are the different amounts consistent?
3. Is there a reasonable grace period, such as ten days, before a penalty is charged for late rent?
4. Is a percentage of the rent charged based on sales?

Empire Management Co.
Rental Invoice

Joe's Surf Shop
Joe Smith
4728 Fifth St., Suite B
San Diego, CA

Dear Mr. Smith,
The following represents your July invoice for rent. Note we did have some extraordinary charges for roof repair which we have amortized between you and the other tenants based on a percentage of your net rentable space.

Further, the center's April promotion ran a little over budget so we have backcharged the Tenants Promotional Budget.

One thing further. You exceeded the grace period in paying your rent last month by 4 days so a late charge is indicated. We also appreciated your offer of a new surfboard with a 12-month ding repair warranty in exchange for 2 months' rent but the owner is a golfer and has no interest in taking up surfing.

Sincerely,

P. Jacus

July Rent	$2,000.00
Common Area fees	$ 320.00
Extraordinary Maintenance Fee	$1,321.00
Tenants Promotion Fee	$ 276.00
Extraordinary Promotion Fee	$ 138.00
Late Charge	$ 200.00
Total Due by July 15, 1995	$4,255.00

345 Tenth St.   Los Angeles, CA

Typical rental invoice

How is it audited? Is there a penalty for mistakes? Does it include telephone or mail order sales?

F. Additional Rent

1. Does the rent increase periodically by the increased operating expenses (pro rata share), by the consumer price index (CPI), or by a fixed percentage?
2. When does the rent increase?
3. Is there a maximum cap on the increase?
4. Is the base year specified and what was last year's base amount?
5. Are the base year expenses based on full tenant occupancy, or are they improperly adjusted (for example, are base year real estate taxes low because they are based on an unfinished building)?
6. Must all expenses be reasonable and directly related to the building's operation?
7. Must Landlord keep books and records?
8. Does Tenant have the right to audit Landlord's books and records?
9. Who pays for the audit?
10. How are disputes over increased operating expenses settled? By negotiation; by mediation; by

arbitration; by lawsuits?
11. Does Tenant receive a credit if the operating expenses are reduced or if the paid estimated monthly amounts exceed the actual incurred expenses?
12. Is the CPI defined and what is the base period?

G. Security Deposit

1. Under what circumstances and when is the security deposit returned?
2. Who gets income from the security deposit?

H. Use

Note: The Use provisions in a lease may be the most important aspect of the lease. If you have severe limitations placed on what you can and cannot sell and the nature of your business changes, you could be in big trouble.

1. Try to get as broad a Use clause as possible, such as, "The Tenant can use the premises for any lawful purpose including but not limited to the sale of clothes or toys or computers, etc." Then try to prohibit anybody else from selling the same thing in your center: "Landlord agrees that tenant shall have the exclusive right to sell clothes or toys or computers, etc., in this shopping center."
2. Find out the penalty for stepping outside your own Use clause and establish how you can force the Landlord to enforce the Use provisions of your restrictive clauses against other tenants not in compliance.

I. Compliance with Laws

1. If tenant must comply with various laws, does Landlord warrant and guarantee that the Premises are in compliance with those laws at the commencement date?
2. Is Tenant's obligation limited to those laws that pertain to the manner in which Tenant will use The Premises?
3. Is Tenant obligated to make structural repairs?
4. Is there a dollar limit on Tenant's obligation?

J. Services and Utilities

1. Which party provides and pays for such services as heating, ventilating and air conditioning (HVAC), electric lighting, water, janitorial and other services?
2. Are the services provided during holidays? What hours of service are excluded?
3. What standard governs Landlord's provisions for HVAC? The standard for first class retail buildings in the area; Landlord's sole discretion, as the weather warrants; in sufficient (or reasonable) amounts and at temperatures sufficient for Tenant's comfortable use and occupancy?
4. What standard governs Landlord's provision of janitorial services? Five days a week; during or after work hours; the standard for first class retail buildings in the area; to a degree deemed sufficient by Landlord?

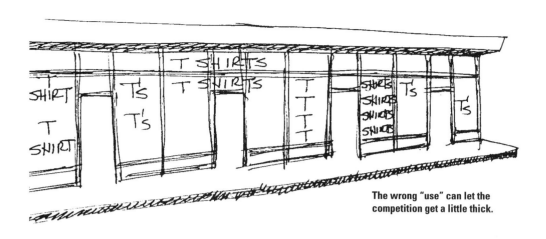

The wrong "use" can let the
competition get a little thick.

Are the janitorial services specified, such as sweeping the sidewalks, striping the parking lot, etc.?
5. What remedies does Tenant have if the services are interrupted? Can these remedies include money damages, rent abatement, and lease cancellation?
6. Is Tenant automatically entitled to the remedies or is Tenant entitled to them only if one or more of the following occurs: the interruption is caused by Landlord's negligence or intentional act; the causes were not beyond the Landlord's reasonable control; or the Landlord failed to use its best efforts (or reasonable efforts or reasonable diligence) to restore the services promptly?

K. Repairs and Maintenance
1. Is Tenant's liability for repair or maintenance or both any greater than keeping The Premises in good order and condition, and to return The Premises at lease termination in the same condition as received at the commencement, except for ordinary wear and tear, damage by the elements, fire, and other unavoidable casualty?

2. If Tenant's obligation is greater than that stated in K.1., does the obligation include responsibility for the structural portions of the building, roof, exterior walls, and systems (HVAC, electrical, mechanical, plumbing, and water) even if Tenant does not have access to them?
3. If Landlord has an obligation to repair, is the obligation to repair with reasonable promptness or in a reasonable time after receiving written notice?

L. Alterations
1. May alterations be made with Landlord's consent or without consent if the alterations cost less than a certain dollar amount?
2. At the Lease's termination, does Landlord have the option of keeping and owning the alterations and trade fixtures added by Tenant, or of having Tenant remove same and repairing the damage?

M. Insurance
1. Do Tenant's policy coverage and limits meet the minimums required by the lease?
2. May Tenant use a blanket or umbrella insurance policy that covers, in addition to The Premises, other premises owned or leased by Tenant?

N. Waiver of Subrogation
1. Is the waiver mutual, that is, is the waiver by Landlord and Tenant?
2. Does Tenant's insurance policy permit the waiver?

O. Indemnity and Hold Harmless Provisions
1. If Tenant must indemnify and hold Landlord harmless from claims, damages, or injuries arising out of Tenant's occupancy of the Premises, what is the degree of Tenant's responsibility? Is Tenant responsible for any and all claims?

P. Landlord's Liability
1. Under what circumstances is Landlord liable to the Tenant? Those arising from Landlord's intentional or negligent acts or omissions?

Q. Casualty
1. If the Demised Premises are damaged by casualty, is Landlord's obligation to repair and restore them as soon as reasonably possible or to use due to diligence?
2. Does Tenant's rent obligation abate from the date the Premises or access thereto are damaged or impaired, and remain abated until the damage is repaired?
3. Is the rent abated in proportion to the nature and extent of damages, impairment of the use that Tenant can reasonably make of the Demised Premises, or in proportion to amount of unusable square feet?
4. May Tenant cancel the Lease if Landlord fails to repair or anticipates being unable to repair The Premises within a reasonable time, such as 90 days?

R. Condemnation
1. Is this provision limited to a taking of part or all of The Premises and access thereto, or does it also include a taking of part or all of the building,

common areas, and parking lot?

2. Is rent abated from the date of the taking?

3. May Tenant terminate the Lease if, as is reasonably determined by Tenant, all or part of The Premises is taken or access is impaired?

4. If the Lease is terminated, is Tenant reimbursed for prepaid rent and other prepaid expenses?

5. Is Tenant entitled to a condemnation award for Tenant's trade fixtures, other property, moving expenses, business dislocation damages, and the unamortized cost of lease hold improvements?

S. Assignment and Subleasing

If for any reason you have to vacate the space, you may want to sublet to whomever you desire as soon as possible. Remember that you will be responsible for the rent whether you are using the space or not, so find out:

1. Is Tenant prohibited from assigning or subleasing the Lease without the prior written consent of Landlord?

2. What standard governs Landlord's decision to consent? Landlord's sole discretion; consent shall not be unreasonably withheld or unduly delayed; or objective reasonable criteria, such as the subtenant's financial strength and nature of its business?

3. Must Tenant obtain consent for an assignment to an affiliated company, and is "affiliated" defined?

T. Default

1. Is vacating or abandoning the premises a default even if Tenant continues paying for the rent?

2. Is Tenant's failure to pay the rent a default only after the rent is more than ten days overdue and Tenant receives written notice of the failure to pay?

3. Is Tenant's failure to comply with other material terms in the Lease a default even if Tenant cures the material breach within 30 days of receiving written notice of the breach?

4. Are the following events: bankruptcy, receivership, seizure of assets, and assignment for the benefit of creditors, automatic defaults only if those events are not corrected within a reasonable time after those events occur?

U. Remedies

1. Before exercising its remedies, must Landlord give Tenant notice or make a demand for cure?

2. Must Landlord mitigate damages, such as by making reasonable efforts to relet?

V. Brokers' Fees

1. Has Tenant dealt with any broker other than the broker specifically mentioned in the Lease, whose fee is payable by Landlord?

W. Quiet Possession

1. Does Landlord warrant Tenant's "quiet possession?"

X. Rules and Regulations

1. Do any current rules or regulations promulgated by Landlord, or Landlord's right to promulgate future rules and regulations, interfere with Tenant's intended business use such as hours of use?

Y. Renewal/Holdover/Options

1. Is the Lease automatically renewed unless either party gives notice of termination?

2. Does Tenant have one or more options to extend the term for one or more years on the same terms and conditions, with the exception of rent, as those found in the original Lease?

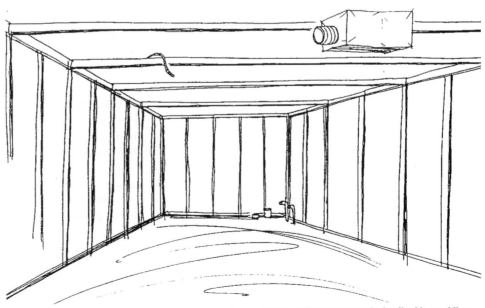

Know what tenant improvements the landlord is providing.

3. Is the rent during the option terms renegotiated or increased by a fixed percentage, the CPI increase, fixed dollar amount, or current market rate?

Z. Improvements

Tenant improvement allowances will substantially impact the cost of your store and should be negotiated sharply. After reading this book you should have an idea of what expenses will be incurred in the store's build out. Some of these expenses may be picked up by the Landlord. In fact, if you are a desirable tenant, the improvement allowance could be 100% of the build-out. Always check:

1. Are all of the proposed improvements itemized on the blueprints and attached as exhibits?

2. If Tenant will pay, after receiving invoices, part of the improvement costs, what portion and how will Tenant pay?

3. If Landlord selects the contractor and Tenant pays part of the costs, what control does Tenant have over the cost? Is competitive bidding required? What if the work is poorly done?

4) If the Landlord will pay for some improvements, how much will he pay and when?

AA. Entire Agreement

1. Is everything Tenant bargained for referenced in the Lease?

BB. Attorney's Fees

1. Is each party entitled to have its attorney's fees paid if it is the prevailing party in any arbitration, litigation, or dispute settled short of litigation, to enforce the Lease?

2. Is the prevailing party also entitled to other reasonable expenses and court costs?

CC. Mechanics' Liens

1. Does Tenant have a reasonable time to discharge the lien before Landlord is able to pay the lien and bill Tenant?

DD. Right to Enter

1. Exclusive of emergencies, must Landlord give Tenant reasonable advance notice of entry?

2. May Landlord enter to inspect, make repairs, construct improvements, or show the Demised Premises to prospective tenants (such as in the last three months of the lease term only)?

3. During Landlord's entry, is Tenant entitled to damages, or rent abatement, for injury caused by Landlord's negligence or unreasonable interference with the conduct of Tenant's business?

EE. Right to First Refusal

(**Note:** Always try to get a right of first refusal on any adjacent spaces.)

1. Is the space sufficiently identified?

2. Is Tenant given written notice of the proposed terms and conditions and a reasonable time, such as 30 days, to respond to the offer?

FF. Tenant's Personal Guarantee

1. Does Tenant's financial strength and size negate Landlord's need for this provision?

GG. Merchants Association

1. Is there a Merchants Association?

2. How is it paid for?

3. What criteria is used to determine how much money the Association will collect and spend, and how it will be spent?

4. What are the penalties for not paying dues and assessments?

As stated earlier, this checklist does not cover every aspect of every retail lease you might encounter, but it should give you a head start in putting the necessary chinks in any standard lease's armor.

Notes

3 WORKING WITH DESIGNERS

To develop an appropriate store plan, most retailers have several choices. The first is to try to do the design work themselves. Many of our clients are ex-jocks, administrators or managers, not designers or retailers. When they do their own design work, it always shows. The colors don't work, the equipment doesn't fit, the displays are a hodgepodge, and what's worse, they don't realize that the store is losing sales simply because of its design and merchandising.

ARCHITECTS OR INTERIOR DECORATORS?

When and if a prospective retailer does realize she needs help, the most frequent person turned to is an architect. The only problem with this option is that again, most architects have absolutely no experience as either retailers or store designers, so one winds up with a store that looks nice, but doesn't sell goods.

Interior decorators are usually the next design choice. Since virtually no regulatory control exists over decorators in most states, anybody with some sense of style (any style) can hang out a shingle as a decorator. As seen before, if the decorator has no retail experience the same problem develops as with the architect: cute store/no sales.

What can you do? First, if you have the money, hire an architect or designer who has designed, through construction, at least 20 stores and not necessarily

your particular type of retail store. Why 20 stores? Because it's too easy to draw something that on a plan looks great, but in the field can't be built, isn't cost-effective, or does not work from a merchandising standpoint. Designers only learn from their mistakes when a project is actually built.

WORKING WITH STORE DESIGNERS

A store designer is not someone who merely creates a pretty store. Rather, it is someone who can create a selling environment within the space, size, look and budgetary constraints placed on the project by the owner. Often the expectations of the retailer are not in touch with the realities of the marketplace. Many times I have had a client express the desire for a beautiful 2000-square-foot store, totally unique, with state-of-the-art lighting, signage, equipment and flooring, all to be accomplished on a budget of $10,000 or less.

An experienced designer understands costs before the project begins, not after the plans have been drawn. He or she has been involved with every aspect of retail design including construction, equipment and merchandising, and will know how to fit the pieces together to create a store that looks good and sells merchandise. Building code knowledge is also essential since in many cases the plans drawn will have to be submitted to a city agency for plan review.

DESIGNHOUSE
COMMERCIAL AND RETAIL DESIGN

Client: Joe Smith
Project: Joe's Surf Shop

Dear Mr. Smith,

The following is our contract to provide you plans for the remodeling of your new store. We will provide you with the following:

1) A set of blueprints indicating:
   a) Floor plans and elevations indicating all merchandising fixtures, dressing rooms, new demising walls, and required demolition.
   b) A reflected ceiling and lighting plan with switching, light placement and fixtures detailed.
   c) All Title 24 calculations.
   d) Storefront signage details.
   e) Color, flooring and finish specifications.
   f) All notes required by the city to obtain a building permit.
   g) A rendering of the store for submission to the landlord.

2) The plans will substantially conform with the California Energy Code Title 24 requirements. An Electrical Engineer may need to be retained by the owner to ensure compliance and to compute required allowances for the building department. If so, DESIGNHOUSE will inform the owner and shall obtain an estimate of engineering costs prior to retaining the Engineer.

3) A budget estimate of the cost of all products per the design supplied by DESIGNHOUSE. After review, this budget estimate will be resubmitted to the Owner in the form of a final cost analysis.

4) In no event shall the total cost of the plans for this project exceed $5,000.00, plus the cost of engineering calculations, without the Owner's consent. We bill at $50.00 per hour plus expenses (long distance calls, blueprints, etc). You will receive a regular billing detailing time and costs incurred.

5) DESIGNHOUSE requires a 33% deposit on the estimated budget prior to beginning the initial drawings. The balance shall be billed every 10 days and the final billing shall be paid on delivery of the final set of drawings.

6) In order to facilitate the services delineated herein, DESIGNHOUSE requires from the Owner:
   A) A complete, up-to-date, set of project's previous working drawings.
   B) The Shopping Center tenants' manual.

7) Other Provisions:
Owner is responsible for obtaining all permits required for this project by the governing authorities.

DESIGNHOUSE is not responsible for any deviations or changes by others to the drawings or specifications provided, without written authorization.

This contract represents the entire agreement between the parties. Any disputes will be handled through Arbitration.

Accepted: _____   Accepted: _____
Owner: Joe Smith   DESIGNHOUSE: K. Tenuta

Typical Shortform Design Contract

DESIGNHOUSE
COMMERCIAL AND RETAIL DESIGN

Joe's Surf Shop
Joe Smith
4728 Fifth. St., Suite B
San Diego, CA

Dear Joe:

The following represents our invoice for July. We have completed the conceptual drawings and are now pulling together the permit set of plans. These should be done by August 15.

I do appreciate how helpful you have been on this job and it has progressed as we anticipated. I will, however, need the outstanding June bill brought current prior to turning over the final set of plans.

We also appreciated your offer of a new surfboard with a 12-month ding repair warranty in exchange for design fees, but I'm a tennis player and have no interest in taking up surfing.

Sincerely,

K. Tenuta
Design Director

Invoice:

12 hrs.	Conceptual development	$50.00 hr.	$600.00
4 hrs.	Lighting Plan	$50.00 hr.	$200.00
1.5 hrs.	Site visit, field measure	$50.00 hr.	$ 75.00
Bill out	Electric engineer, title 24 calculations $250.00	$250.00	
Travel	54 miles, 20¢ per	$ 10.80	$ 10.80
Phone	Long distance	$ 2.40	$ 2.40
Copy	4 sets blue prints $5.40	$ 22.00	
Total			$1160.20
Past due balance		$1350.00	
Total Due			$2510.20

Typical Design Invoice

Poorly drawn blueprints will require numerous resubmissions to the city, each costing you money as your rented but uninhabited space lies dormant awaiting a building permit.

A well-designed store has blueprints that are easy to read so a contractor doesn't have to pad his estimate to cover all the things he really didn't understand. A knowledgeable planner takes advantage of "off the shelf" equipment so fixture costs are minimized. A competent designer understands colors, finishes, lighting, flooring, cabinet work, HVAC systems, ceiling tiles, fireproofing, etc. The store doesn't have to be redesigned in midstream to meet deadlines, budgets, codes or design review board criteria.

Finally, a retail designer can create a store that allows sufficient room for merchandising all your goods while still looking not only attractive, but also interesting, fun and exciting. The kind of store that people want to come back to and, in fact, will consider one of their "favorite stores."

How do you find an experienced retail space planner? Frankly, there are not many around. There are designers and architects available who have been involved with store plans, but very few who day in, day out, work only on retail projects. Of the designers who do specialize in retail planning, most have a particular *forte*. Some design sporting goods stores, others women's apparel, while others design drug, gift or auto shops. How do you find them? Ask. Ask shop owners. Find stores that you like and seek out the designers. Always find out the budget given the designer to create the space. A store that just looks pretty good may look exceptional when you find out the budget was only $7500.

ELEMENTS IN SPECIALTY and THEME STORES

Toys and Kids' Clothes
- Tinker Toy fixtures, racks, shelves
- Wooden soldier mannequins
- Building block pedestals and platforms
- Play area
- Kids' videos
- Kids' photo blow-ups
- Circus squiggle mirror
- Neon balloons

Auto Parts and Accessories
- Display a car outfitted with specialty parts. Or take part of the car and do the same thing, such as the front of a car showing engine accessories.
- Racing photo blow-ups
- Seat display with actual seats on pedestals
- Stereo sound in simulated auto cockpit (seats, dash, etc.)

Old Country
- Wood antique fixtures
- Armoires, lawyer's bookcases, wicker chairs,
- Wallpaper
- Brass hardware fittings
- Carpet inlays/wood floor
- Indirect lighting
- Recessed ceiling/tin inlays
- Ferns and light palms

Art Galleries
- Low voltage spot lamps. Track and recessed lighting.
- Mixed flooring (carpet, wood, tile)
- Multiple pedestals, mixed sizes
- Dark ceiling
- Mixed wall finishes (paint, brick, slatwall, grid)

Active Sports (surf, sail, ski)
- Active look or flexible mannequins
- Action photo blow-ups
- Vendor banners/neon brand I.D.
- Sport related video
- Multiple merchandising methods
- Rack-bin-shelf-speciality slat or grid wall
- Bright lights with spots
- Large dressing rooms with mirrors

Hardware
- Extensive signage and explanatory graphics
- Video how-to's
- Demonstration area
- Multiple merchandising methods:
- Slatwall backed gondolas, grids, slatwall pinwheels, tier tables
- Book area with seating
- How-to video rental
- Project photo blow-ups

Card and Gift
- Multiple level and method merchandising
- Slatwall or grid towers, H's, Z's, pinwheels
- Tier tables/platforms with and without plex tops
- Tiered card racks on slatwall or grid
- Mixed floor finishes
- Neon-banner-truss in upper elevations
- Impulse oriented check-out
- Showcase, tier display, slatwall merchandiser

High-volume, low-end, discount stores
- Bright fluorescent lights, no-spot lights
- Patterned linoleum floor
- Hand-written or very bright signs
- Clothing racks should be round or double bar
- Sale and dump tables in droves

Theme Stores

50's
- Juke box/music
- Hot rod/motorcycle
- Diner with stools
- Sales uniforms/jeans, skirts, bobby sox
- Pictures of movie stars, James Dean, etc.
- Linoleum floor
- Lots of chrome and neon

Beach
- 1956 Ford Woody
- Sand in the window displays
- Volley ball net display
- Palm trees
- Lifeguard towers
- Thatched roof dressing room and counter
- Beach/surf posters
- Sales uniforms/shorts, Hawaiian shirts

Jungle
- An old Jeep
- Vines, bamboo trees
- Jungle music
- Netting
- Stuffed artificial jungle animals
- Natural wood fixtures, crates, etc.
- Jungle photos
- Sales uniforms/safari shorts, hats, vest

Jewelry Stores and Sections
- Showcases should be a combination of sit-down, wall and pedestal.
- Flooring must be high-end. Try carpet and marble.
- Lighting should be predominantly track and/or recessed halogen low voltage spots and fluorescents with diffusers.
- Small backlit photos will sell merchandise.
- Create interest in the showcase displays by using small risers to support the merchandise at various heights.

Shoe Stores
- Seating must be comfortable and clean. Buy quality chairs.
- Use full length mirrors, not just foot mirrors.
- Mix merchandising with shoes shown a few at a time, and individually.
- Lights should be a mix of incandescent spots and diffused fluorescents.
- Create interest in the shoes displays by using risers to support the merchandise at various heights.

Men and Women's Apparel
- Pick a store style
- Country, contemporary, elegant, high-tech, eclectic
- Light with care, mix fluorescents, spot lamps
- Mix flooring but let carpet predominate
- Big dressing rooms, mirrors, seats, lights
- Multiple level and method merchandising
- Wall merchandising should allow waterfalls, shoulder-out hanging, shelving, or specialty display
- Use presentation racks, 2-way, 4-way, slatwall H's, Z's, pinwheels, tier tables, binning systems
- Impulse oriented check-out
- Showcase, slatwall merchandiser
- Multiple mirrors
- Photo blow-ups for some stores
- Keep most colors neutral

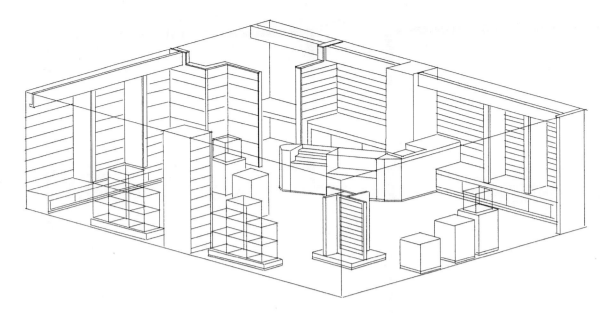

Don't limit yourself to local designers. Most design work is done on paper so other than a preliminary visit to meet the clients and see the shop site, often a designer can create a store from many miles away.

WHAT WILL IT COST?

What should you pay for a designer? Most charge about $75 to $95 per hour. We find that the average 1500 to 2500-square-foot shop comes in at around $1.50 to $3.50 per square foot to design, with a price variance based on the work required. In many cases, permits are not required and the only plans you will need are a floor plan, color and finish specs, and fixture detailing, so the price is at the low end of the scale. However, add elevations, cabinet details, lighting plans, signs, logos, storefronts, permit requirements, HVAC engineering, etc., and the price escalates very rapidly.

It is important to first find out what your city requires in the way of plans and permits. It might be possible to plan the store in a manner that avoids the requirement of a permit and the attendant drawings that are required for same. Then learn exactly what you are going to get from your designer. If a permit is not required, the designer's fee should be much lower than if the permit is needed. Get a cost on everything the designer will prepare so you don't fall into a state of shock when the bill arrives.

WHAT TO EXPECT

Here are some of the drawings you can expect to get from a design firm:

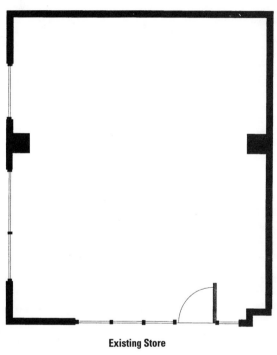

Existing Store

1) The floor and elevation plan, including all fixtures
2) Lighting and ceiling plans with load calculations
3) Heating, ventilating and air conditioning plans
4) Plumbing and electric plans
5) Storefront and signage
6) Fixture and cabinet detail
7) Finish details including colors for paint, laminate, flooring, awnings, fixtures, etc.
8) Renderings of the actual store

Many stores, particularly those in an existing location, don't require nearly as much detail as a new freestanding or mall shop. Keep in mind that any work that needs a permit requires at least simple drawings indicating what you are planning to do and how you plan to accomplish it. Without the appropriate details, you will not be able to get a permit to build.

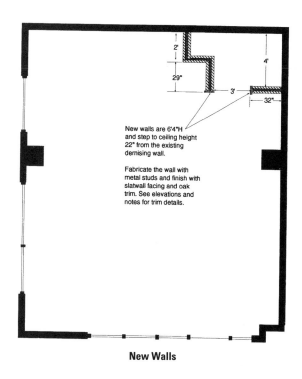

New walls are 6'4"H and step to ceiling height 22" from the existing demising wall.

Fabricate the wall with metal studs and finish with slatwall facing and oak trim. See elevations and notes for trim details.

New Walls

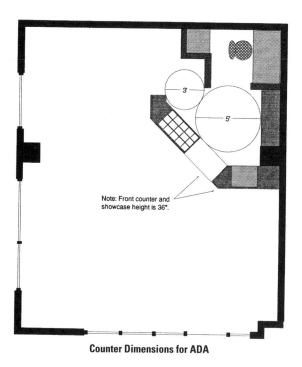

Note: Front counter and showcase height is 36".

Counter Dimensions for ADA

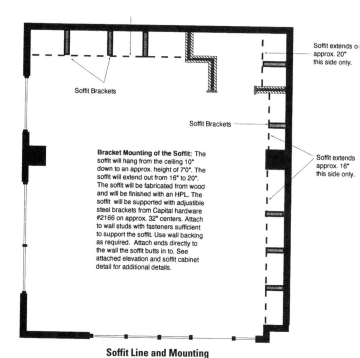

Soffit extends o approx. 20" this side only.

Soffit Brackets

Soffit Brackets

Soffit extends approx. 16" this side only.

Bracket Mounting of the Soffit: The soffit will hang from the ceiling 10" down to an approx. height of 7'0". The soffit will extend out from 16" to 20". The soffit will be fabricated from wood and will be finished with an HPL. The soffit will be supported with adjustible steel brackets from Capital hardware #2166 on approx. 32" centers. Attach to wall studs with fasteners sufficient to support the soffit. Use wall backing as required. Attach ends directly to the wall the soffit butts in to. See attached elevation and soffit cabinet detail for additional details.

Soffit Line and Mounting

Further, you won't be able to understand what you are paying to have built.

Aside from the drawings, what an accomplished store designer will provide you is a store that sells goods, not one that merely looks good. You will get a store that is relatively easy to build and, most important, a store that works well within the budget parameters you have set. Lastly you should get a store that pays for its design fee many times over in sales through the years.

WORKING WITH SHOPFITTERS

What is the alternative to a store designer or an architect? A store equipment firm or, as the profession is called in Europe, a shopfitter. Remember what I said earlier. A designer makes money selling his or her time. On the other hand, a professional who sells store equipment can stretch profit margins across design, construction, equipment and display merchandising. This allows the shopfitter to sometimes fund a retail project a little more closely than the merchant could have done by going to each trade separately. Further, a shopfitter has usually been involved with hundreds of stores and is aware of shortcuts that will save money across the board in the store's creation.

If the shopfitter you hire is experienced in retail construction, he or she will understand the necessity of

getting the store opened as expeditiously as possible. Due to seasonal prerequisites (Christmas, summer, ski season, etc.) time can mean quick earnings (or losses) and the contractor who can get you open the quickest may be the one who will make you the most money.

When hiring a store fixture company to design your store, look at what they have done in the past. Most fixture companies are interested in selling you the line of fixtures they either distribute or manufacture so

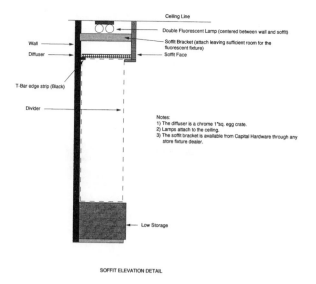

Soffit Elevation Detail

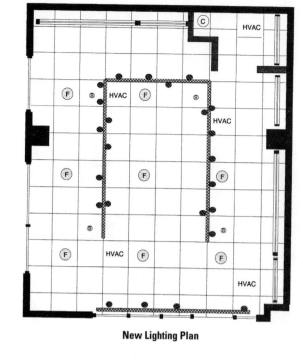

New Lighting Plan

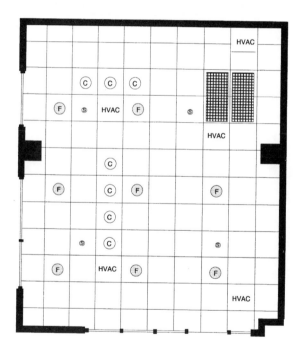

Existing Ceiling

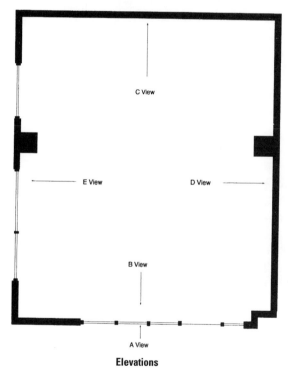

Elevations

some of their store plans may be oriented toward their standard fixtures rather than custom cabinets or displays. Further, the firm will usually not charge for floor layouts so the plans may not be as complete as those submitted by a professional designer. However, if your storefitting and construction budget is less then $10,000, by the time you are done with the basic build-out, flooring, lighting, signage and merchandising requirements, you will have little enough money left for fixtures, much less design fees.

To summarize, hire a design firm or store fixture specialist with experience to ensure your store is designed to sell merchandise, open on time and within budget. Let its staff know what you have in mind and make sure you tell them how much money you have to spend. Most importantly, don't be afraid to provide plenty of input into the design process. *It's your money, your investment of time and your future business. Make sure you protect it.*

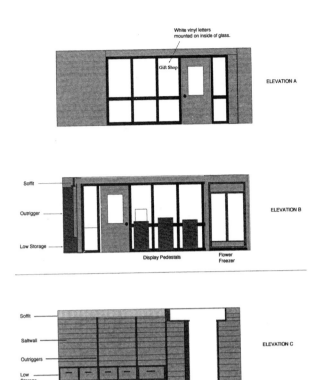

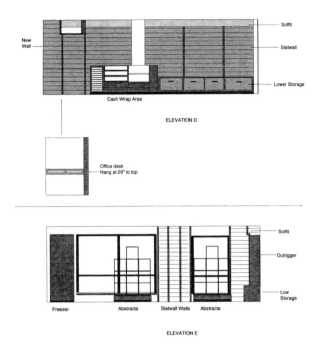

DEVELOP A STORE THEME

Whether you work with a design firm or a fixture company, it is important that a store theme be established early in the developmental process. The *look* of the store will impact all design decisions including the storefront, signage, finish materials, fixtures and merchandising format.

With the designer, develop a store look and merchandising methodology. Do you want an old fashion wood and brass style or do you like high-tech space frames with neon and chrome? You can strive for a very clean, contemporary look much like The Gap or try to create a theme motif like Banana Republic. In both cases the goal is to create a store that people want to shop. What you want to hear them say when they enter is, "This is a great looking store. Looks like it has some wonderful merchandise. Let's spend some time here."

To that end, the store's style might be old fashioned, high-tech or simply very contemporary, but in any event it must be done correctly. The lighting, colors, flooring and display equipment should all work together to create an attractive, comfortable store that presents your merchandise in a manner that attracts attention and promotes sales. That style will serve as the backdrop to all your merchandising efforts, so spend serious time on its development and integration into your store's overall concept.

Further, the store must appeal to the market for your merchandise. Are you selling to men, women, young, old, moms, dads, specialists in a field, tourists, people in a hurry or with leisure time? Do you have a lot of competition or are you the only game in town (for now)? Are you a discount store or a specialty shop? Try to determine your customer in advance so that much of the ambiance and merchandising is directed toward that type of buyer.

Try to differentiate your store from any other you've ever seen. Sure, you can utilize elements from other shops such as colors, particular lights, carpet styles and methods of display presentation, but put those elements together in a way that is clearly your own. Do something, anything, that is tasteful, different and fun, so when people come into your store they really decide that they like it. Be interesting, distinct, and original.

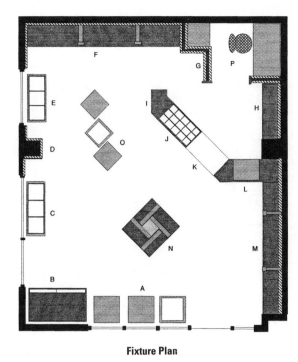

Fixture Plan

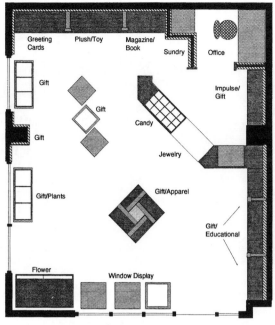

Preliminary Merchandising

But let the designer know this is your goal and make sure he or she is given the budget to support it.

All of these questions are factors that must be taken into account in the initial design phase so that the final juxtaposition of product, clientele and retail environment work in harmony to do one thing: profitably sell merchandise.

INVESTING IN DESIGN

There is a secondary reason to invest in an exciting store. Yes, you will sell more goods. But beyond that, developers are always looking for stores that have an edge, stores that attract customers and bring traffic to their center. Remember that the rents a developer can charge are based on location and the continuing retail success of the center's tenants. If a center doesn't attract profitable lessees, it will lose customers and eventually, rental income. So, developers are always looking for "hot" tenants. If you look successful and show "the retail edge," developers will seek you out. They will offer you space in quality locations and they will give you tenant improvement allowances that in many cases are never amortized back into the lease.

If you plan to expand, design a store that attracts customers and landlords.

One thing further. Many of my clients spend years building their retail stores only to find when they do try to sell the business that its value has more to do with the existing leases than the annual cash flow or sales volume. If you can set up multiple locations, in terrific locations, with long term leases or options, the value of your business will increase well beyond its intrinsic value as a retail operation. The store must look right to be offered those types of locations. Make sure it does.

Projected entry allows easy title browsing.

4 STOREFRONT AND SIGN CONSIDERATIONS

When planning a new store, our analysis of the internal layout is closely associated with the look and feel customers will get when viewing the outside of the store. How will people know you exist? The storefront, the identification sign and the display windows. Window display is discussed at length in the merchandising section of this book, but the windows are only part of the overall presentation your store makes when first seen by a potential customer. The storefront finish materials, size and shape, as well as the store's identification sign all have a bearing on the impression created in the minds of those passing by.

Is the store fun, serious, a discount operation or very "high end?" A shop with small display windows, pinpoint lighting and a single-entry door may indicate high-priced merchandise, while a large, open entry invites customers into the store. Tall windows with exotic mannequins on platforms will usually keep the budget buyer away, while a brightly lit, deep window, full of handwritten sale signs will pull those discounters right through the front door.

In most cases, a small retailer has very little control over the configuration or architectural detailing involved in his storefront. If you are locating in a strip center, the developer has already built out the fronts and in fact will be telling you exactly how your storefront will look and perhaps your signage as well. The only design latitude available will be the window displays. On the other hand, if you are going into a mall, the storefront will be yours to design as long as you can get it past design review and you can afford it.

Most current design trends are leaning toward smaller entries with exciting window displays and interesting sign work. The '80s concept of wide-open storefronts has been refined to build intimacy with the customer as well as control security.

THE WINDOWS

I suggest that if you are going into a mall, you analyze the need to define your image within that retail center. Sporting goods shops often sell both equipment and apparel so it is important that you leave room in the windows for mannequins and display props that tell your shop's story better than any similar store in the mall.

Plan your front windows by imagining just what you are going to put on display. How much room do you need and what type of display will you be doing? Spend time in other shopping centers and malls before you make any kind of decision. Get ideas and relay them to your design firm. Finally, make sure that you have gone over the tenant manual carefully so that what is designed can be implemented.

STOREFRONT MATERIALS

Storefront materials in a strip center are usually

Kid's stuff comes in many sizes. This window provides enough room to tell a "story."

Combination of neon and backlit plastic channels.

High -tech, interesting front.

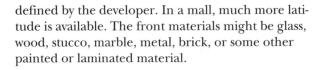

defined by the developer. In a mall, much more latitude is available. The front materials might be glass, wood, stucco, marble, metal, brick, or some other painted or laminated material.

Many stores have incorporated storefront materials or props that tie in to the store's theme. Banana Republic uses jeeps and stuffed animals to sell travel gear; Adventure 16's storefront uses a tent as an awning and real logs, trees and boulders to market their camping and trekking gear. A Laize Adzer will use stucco and tile to sculpt Eastern palace walls surrounding the front windows and entry, while Laura Ashley or Polo will use wood and trim details to impart a posh, English manor feeling.

With these types of themes, storefront details are not mandatory. In many cases tall windows or an open front might do the trick, but if you are truly trying to be different and to create your own image in the marketplace, the storefront materials and design become very important. The price can be high. Getting away

from a simple glass front requires more design time and contractors, other than glazers. In some cases I have seen the storefront alone represent 25% of the store's total budget.

SIGN DESIGN

Sign designs, sizes and finishes are usually mandated to some degree, by the city building department, and in many cases the Landlord. However, within the parameters defined, a designer can usually come up with a sign that captures the public's attention, a sign that creates a store image before the customer steps in the front door. Neon can look young and hip, awning signs trendy and "cool," back-lighted plastic box signs may create a discount image, while a hand-lettered, wood-burned redwood sign may create that upscale feeling. All in a sign? You bet.

The importance of sign design will vary based on store location. In a strip center, the sign style is usually mandated by the landlord, so what the sign says is much more important than how it looks. Quite often a strip center location is some distance from passing traffic so your sign must explain just what it is you're selling. Ocean Enterprises is a San Diego-based dive retailer with locations in several strip centers. All their exterior signs have large, uniform letters, that state, "Dive Shop." Why? What's an Ocean Enterprise? In a strip center, make sure your sign tells what you sell because drive-by traffic often cannot see your front window displays.

Street-side stores do well with signs that are easy to read, unique and self explanatory. People drive by quickly. Attract their attention and inform them of your existence. If your store's name is not product evident, either spell out what you are selling on the storefront or make sure your windows do.

AWNINGS

Lettered awnings attract interest while allowing the retailer to push his store out over the lease line closer to the street. Awnings also serve as sunshields protecting merchandise in storefront windows and as a way to brighten an otherwise dull front facade. Further, for some reason people are simply attracted to stores with awnings. Maybe it is the shade provided, or memories of romantic movie scenes under awnings, but for whatever reason people are attracted to these canvas appendages. Use one over your windows if it works well with the rest of the design and fits the budget.

Awnings always attract attention.

NEON

Add neon in the window to really create interest. Try a neon sign, or outline the windows, or play with geometric shapes, or zig zag down one side, or try neon lines running out the front window, over the face of the building and disappearing onto the roof. Get creative. Carry the look into the store with a neon logo over the counter or across the back wall so drive-by customers can see it. Use two colors that complement each other such as purple and green, or turquoise and lavender. If colors are wild, so too can be the store's look. However, don't overkill with neon in a small store. The light is so bright it will cast its color over your merchandise.

MALL SIGNS

If you are in a mall, the sign must be different and interesting. Mall stores are very competitive with each other and must go the extra mile to lure customers into their store, in many cases for the first time and absent any pre-

vious advertising. The sign can be a part of that lure. Several years ago, we were involved in the design of a hat store called Gotcha Covered. The sign was fabricated from canvas to look like the side of a baseball cap 4 feet high and 8 feet long, including the brim. Nobody passed that store without stopping and looking in.

Mall signs don't have to be too exotic, but they must be graphically interesting, well composed and fabricated, and not take up so much of the storefront that they block the display windows, where the action should really be.

SIGN COSTS

Most sign companies have in-house graphics departments, so before you drop a couple thousand dollars on logo design, talk to some sign people. They may be able to design a sign for you with a logo you can use in the rest of your business. Further, if the logo is to be designed by the sign company, you may save a little over having it designed elsewhere.

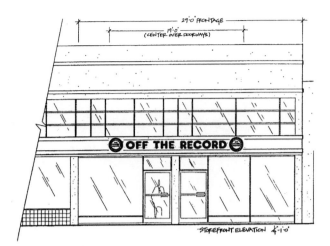

The sign is a combination of open channel metal letters and neon.

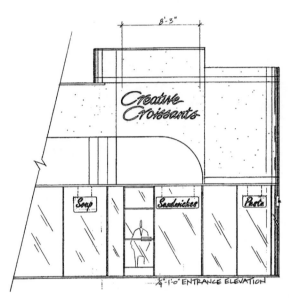

Neon logo sign and window product info.

A sign's price will vary dramatically depending upon the type, finish and length of message you are trying to get across. The price is most directly tied to the finish materials being used. Complex signs involving a long time to fabricate will also cost more.

Signs are normally fabricated from:
• Individual metal and plastic letters that are back lighted.
• Back-lighted boxes that hold double sheets of plastic. The front sheet is cut out in the shape of the store's name or logo to allow for light to shine through the lower sheet.
• Neon.
• Wood, either carved, sandblasted, or painted.
• Cut foam letters with metal or plastic laminate faces
• Cut vinyl letters attached to wood, plastic or metal

Pricing usually follows the same format with the individual letters the most expensive and the vinyl sign the least expensive.

If you are not located in a mall (most malls won't let you do this) and want to save a considerable amount of money on your sign work, consider mounting and painting a wooden sign board on your storefront. Use a simple neon logo I.D. sign and computer cut-out vinyl letters to tell the rest of the shop's story. You will need to externally light the face of the sign but the dollar savings can be quite large.

The vinyl letters are available though most sign firms and come prespaced, so you can mount them yourself. In fact, some of my clients have simply used vinyl letters directly on the storefront windows in lieu of any other sign and allowed the interior illumination to serve as a backlight.

SUMMARY
The storefront brings your customers in, so plan it accordingly. As a budget priority, it is at the high end of the list. If your budget is low, focus on the window displays and sign. If you have a little more latitude, incorporate the theme of the store into the overall storefront concept.

In any event, get the sign work bid by several firms to ensure correct pricing. One last sign tip: a major criterion in pricing signs is the amount of letters involved. If you plan to open a few stores, you might keep your store's name short and sweet.

5 STORE LAYOUT & COLORS

My design department has been involved in the planning of many stores over the last thirteen years and several years ago it became evident we needed to develop a formula that could be used in each case to set the parameters of the design process. After defining the store's style or theme, we use the following program to commence the planning process of each store we are involved with. It is a program that you can follow as well.

The initial design process starts with the size and location of the basic store elements that are generic to virtually every store and include:
1) Size and layout of store shell including doors and windows
2) Location of any immovable building elements
3) Size and location of bathroom
4) Size and location of storage/office area
5) Size and location of dressing rooms
6) Size and location of storefront windows
7) Shape and location of front counter
8) Size and location of any building elements particular

to this specific shop. This might include a rental area, a training room, a repair shop, etc.
9) Store shape and traffic planning
10) Store colors

Once these specific areas are defined, we can move on to next design phase, which includes:
• Merchandising
• Flooring
• Ceiling
• Lighting
• Wall and floor fixtures
• Exterior signage

To begin the process:

THE SHELL
The size and layout of the store shell, including doors and windows, usually will be provided by the landlord. Rarely will there be anything you can do about its configuration. If you are in a strip center, the vanilla shell will normally include a storefront, a finished floor

Typical 20'x60' store in a strip center.

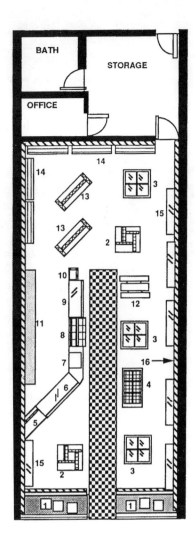

CARD AND GIFT
FIXTURE SCHEDULE
1) DISPLAY PEDESTALS
2) GRID PINWHEEL
3) ABSTARCTA
4) WIRE BINS
5) SLATWALL MERCHANDISER
6) SHOWCASE
7) CASH COUNTER
8) TIER BINNING
9) SHOWCASE
10) SLATWALL TOWER
11) BACK COUNTER
12) TIERED SALE TABLE
13) GRID GONDOLAS
14) PLEX-3 TIER CARD DISPLAY
15) GLASS SHELVES
16) SLATWALL PANELS TO 8'

Typical card and gift store in a strip center.
Walls are predominantly slatwall to promote
maximum flexibility. Floor fixtures are all move-
able and allow for mixed merchandising.

without coverings, sheetrocked and taped walls, fluo-rescent lighting, a ceiling, a bathroom, and a heating and air conditioning system.

If you are in a mall location, you may have control over the storefront within defined parameters, but the mall might not provide you with any of the other basic store elements that you would get in a strip center. It is crucial that you find out just what you are getting in the way of tenant improvements prior to signing the lease and prior to establishing a budget with your designer.

NON-MOVEABLE STORE ELEMENTS
These might include trusses, beams, soffits, etc., that must be incorporated into the store's space planning simply because they are immovable and must be worked around and not through. Make sure you examine the plans of any yet-to-be-built spaces careful-ly before signing a lease. I have, in several cases, had to design around very obtrusive beams and soffits that were unanticipated by the retailer because he signed a

lease prior to the center build-out and without examining the blueprints sufficiently.

THE BATHROOM
Little is usually left to the discretion of the designer in bathroom placement. The plumbing has been preset and the bathroom is going where it is indicated on the center's plan. Most bathrooms in retail establishments must now be built to the handicapped code. This places the size at approximately 7 feet by 9 feet.

THE STORAGE/OFFICE AREA
Here you have a bit of design discretion. Most of my clients prefer that we build a wall across the back of the store and plug in a storage area along with a small private office. Usually, the smaller the storage area, the better. With retail rents running $1 to $5 per foot, most merchants prefer to spend their rental dollars on "selling space" rather than "storage space."

In some cases, due to a predefined architectural ele-ment such as a structural beam or wall, or due to the

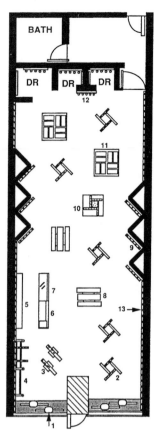

APPAREL AND ACCESSORIES
1) TUBE FORMS
2) 4 WAY RACKS, SLANT & STRAIGHT ARMS
3) 2 WAY RACKS, SLANT & STRAIGHT ARMS
4) TUBE OUTRIGGERS WITH WATERFALLS &
   HANGBAR
5) BACK COUNTER
6) CASH COUNTER
7) SHOWCASE
8) TIER SALE TABLE
9) 2' X 8' WALL GRIDS
10) GRID PINWHEEL
11) GLASS BINS
12) MIRROR WITH LIGHTS ABOVE
13) SLATWALL PANELS TO 8'

Typical clothing store in a strip center. Note walls have been fabricated in the center of the store to attract interest and break up the space. Dressing rooms are in the rear and are still visible from the counter.

requirements of a specialty retailer, we might place the storage area or office in a location other than along the back wall. However, because of the amount of space this type of construction normally takes up in the middle of the store, we are always concerned about the security aspects related to the design. You should be, too. Any walls that give a customer room to hide will ensure increased shrinkage. If a blind spot is created, install mirrors or cameras.

DRESSING ROOMS

Dressing rooms are always a major topic of discussion in the store planning process. Neophyte retailers are convinced that the dressing rooms should be right next to the front counter so potential thefts can be averted. I assume these retailers are convinced that this proximity to the counter will inhibit theft. It won't. If some people want to rip you off and if they are any good at it at all, they will do so even if you stand in the dressing room with them while they are changing.

Locate dressing rooms in the back of the store so customers have to walk through all the merchandise to get to them. Sell some goods along the way. Just

maintain a clear line of sight to the dressing room doors and make the doors short so you can see feet and heads. We normally specify 5-foot-high louvered doors, which we hang 12 inches off the floor. If nothing else, they create an illusory lack of privacy.

Make the dressing rooms comfortable. Minimum size is 3.5 feet by 3.5 feet per room. Put a lock on each door, and a bench, hook, and mirror in each room. Place pictures of outfits or products in the dressing rooms to remind customers of other items they might be interested in. A busy clothing store will require at least three dressing rooms and a large (over 3,000 square feet) store may need more. Keep in mind that many communities require at least one handicapped dressing room with a 60-inch interior circumference and a 36-inch door.

DISPLAY WINDOWS

Exciting windows will attract customers other than those who would have come into your store anyway. I've seen more successful stores built around creative windows than around great merchandise. Make sure you have enough room in the windows to create an effective display.

If possible, build window display platforms at least 30 inches deep (36 to 42 inches if you are using mannequins), raise them off the floor to window height, back them with a wall or a see-through grid and, most importantly, light them well.

Backing the windows is always a big decision for the first-time retailer. The discussion with the store designer usually goes something like this:

Retailer: "I want people to be able to see into my shop, and I want to be able to see out. Let's put up a display platform with no back so the customers can see through."

Designer: "People will look at what is in the window, not at what's behind it. Back the windows with a wall so we can use its back side for additional merchandising. Let's not confuse shoppers by showing a window display that has activity behind it."

The compromise the first time around is usually for a grid backwall that allows frontal display while still letting people see through to the sales floor. The second store usually gets a full or partial backwall behind the window display with merchandising on the back side. People do concentrate on what's in the window, not what's behind it.

COUNTER AREA

Counter location is another "hot spot" with retailers. Many first-time retailers are convinced that the checkout counter should be right next to the front door so customers don't dash out without paying for their merchandise. In fact, most people are more comfortable having a little space to browse around a store prior to hitting the wrap desk. Scout out the locations of check-out counters at The Limited or The Gap, or virtually any major chain store. Most start anywhere from 12 to 20 feet into the store, depending upon the size of the space.

We find that most strip center and mall stores are relatively narrow, so a wall location for the check-out counter becomes the best design choice. In wider stores, an island check-out might be a better choice simply to control traffic flow and monitor customer needs.

To create interest in the wrap area, we often use angled transition cabinets and multiple merchandising fixture elements. The angularity combined with the diversity of product presentation pulls customers around the wrap area, promoting additional sales and attracting customers even deeper into the store. The mixed fixture elements might include:
• The cash wrap with a slatwall face
• A tiered display unit with plex dividing bins
• Half-vision showcases
• A slatwall half-gondola with glass bins
• Angled transition ends with showcase tops

A back counter is usually essential for both storage and as an additional wrapping area. Because an enclosed wrap area can be quite expensive, we often substitute a ledge-backed table top with a single storage shelf below. This can serve the same purpose as an enclosed cabinet at a fraction of the expense.

SPECIAL REQUIREMENTS
Many stores have specialty space needs that must be included in the design. These might include a rental area in a ski shop, a training room in a dive store, a repair area in a golf shop, etc. Plug in the size space required so the rest of the store can be built around it. Plan to utilize the space in such a way that it does not interfere with the traffic flow or create a security problem.

Now, with the basic store elements locked in place, let's proceed on to the other design requirements necessary to complete the store.

STORE SHAPE AND TRAFFIC PATTERNS
The shape of the store has so far been defined by what must be done with the required areas including storage, bathrooms, dressing rooms, etc. With those elements in place we now have the opportunity to design the shape of the walls and the floor layout of the shop to our own specifications.

Wall dimensioning has much to do with budget. It is much more interesting for customers to shop in a store that is not a square or rectangular box with long,

uninterrupted walls. On the other hand, every time a wall is popped out at a 45-degree angle, the carpenter, the sheet rocker, the taper, and the painter, will all come in to spend your money. If budget and space allow, the walls can be angled, soffited and platformed, at various heights and locations, to create interest and multiple display opportunities. Give customers a reason to keep traveling through the store. Make them want to see what's behind that angled wall or on the other side of that platform. Just don't create dead space or security problems with walls that hide people or merchandise.

We do find that most merchants don't have the budget to do much with the shape of the store's interior shell. That extra $2000 to $10,000 for wall dimensioning is better spent on removable store equipment systems that provide much the same look without the expense.

DIRECTING TRAFFIC FLOW
Floor fixtures should be used in conjunction with floorcoverings to encourage and direct traffic flow. Traffic may be directed in a straight line, on an angle,

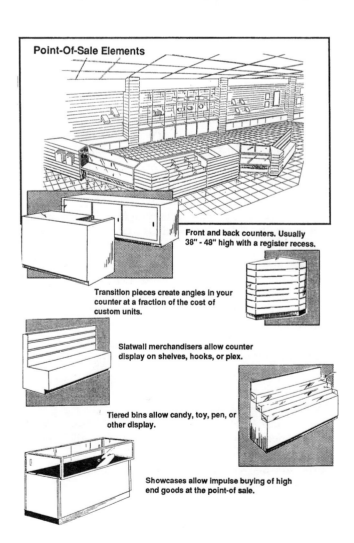

Point-Of-Sale Elements

Front and back counters. Usually 38" - 48" high with a register recess.

Transition pieces create angles in your counter at a fraction of the cost of custom units.

Slatwall merchandisers allow counter display on shelves, hooks, or plex.

Tiered bins allow candy, toy, pen, or other display.

Showcases allow impulse buying of high end goods at the point-of sale.

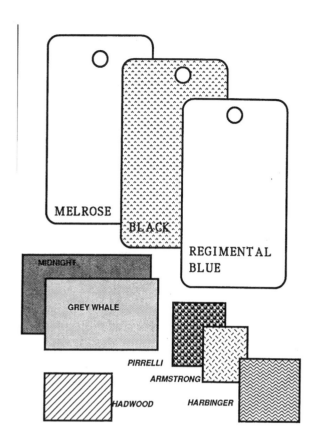

MELROSE

BLACK

REGIMENTAL BLUE

MIDNIGHT

GREY WHALE

PIRRELLI

ARMSTRONG

HADWOOD

HARBINGER

The key in any color program is to remember that the walls, fixtures, ceilings, etc., are merely a backdrop to your merchandise. The colors should define and accentuate the environment of the store without distracting from the impact of the merchandise presentation.

Finish Schedule

Paint
1 Sinclair Grey Whale 437-T
2 Sinclair Midnight 439-V

Cabinet and Slatwall Laminate
3 Nevamar Regimental Blue S-3-16T
4 Nevamar Melrose S-1-33-T
5 Nevamar Black Granite GR-6-1M

Floorcoverings
6 Harbinger Confetti, New Year's
7 Hardwood plank bleached oak
8 Armstrong Vinyl Tile Premium White
9 Pirelli Radial Dot Red

Typical Finish Schedule

around curves—or in a large store, down a pathway—simply by placing your fixtures in a manner that leaves little choice to the customer. The configuration of the traffic flow will vary based upon product and the store's size and shape, but the primary things to keep in mind are:

• Customers should be encouraged to walk through the entire store. Don't put things in their way.

• Leave at least 36 inches of aisle space in any given area of the store and 48 inches for major walkways.

• Leave a clear line of sight to the rear of the store; put something interesting on display along the back wall, and light it. Get people to the back of the store and they will buy things coming and going.

• Don't clog your counter area. Leave at least 48 inches of clear space in front of it.

Remember that there are no hard and fast rules about store layout. We try for flexibility in design and fixtures, so you can change the look and flow of the store as needs dictate.

COLORS
The most frequently asked question in store planning seems to be what colors to use. The answer

varies depending upon the type of merchandise you are selling, who your customers are, the physical dimensions of the store, and what the theme or look of the shop will be.

Sporting goods and kids' stores will support bright, primary colors, although they may clash with many of the apparel colors you now carry. As discussed below, we encourage a neutral background color with a series of dark, punch colors to brighten the store. If the store owner is somewhat traditional or conservative we might go with natural wood and stone finishes. If the look is a little more high-tech, we lean toward dark ceilings, bright walls, and high-intensity punch colors.

If your store is very large, brightly colored banners or graphics against a neutral background will help bring the size of the store into a more intimate scale. If the ceiling is high, dark colors will tend to bring it down. If the room is narrow, light walls will broaden it. Color tricks can and must be used where necessary. However, certain simple rules are always followed. In most cases, we try to specify a field color in a neutral tone to serve as the color base and background for the merchandise. Several other colors are then picked up as accents or "punch" to add interest and detail to the space. Accent colors are used sparingly since we are not trying to compete with the colors in the merchandise.

A neutral color is usually fairly light in tone, such as a beige, gray or off-white. These colors are soothing and non-responsive, and provide the ideal backdrop to most merchandise. Paint companies provide color chip sample cards that show several tones of a color, graduating from light to dark. The lighter tones on most cards can be used as the neutral background so the tone of the store could be blue, green, yellow, depending on the look you are after.

Accent colors can either fall within the same family of colors as the background color or come from of a different area of the palate all together. Try a beige field color with teal accents or gray with light yellow accents, or salmon with gray. The color combinations are endless and must be tied to the individual store. Work with a designer on your colors just to ensure compatibility. Once the carpet is down and the fixtures in place, it will be a while before you can change your mind.

Color opportunities in a store include:
• Floorcoverings
• Walls
• Ceiling
• Lights
• Fixtures and displays
• Graphics
• Storefront and sign

To cover them one at a time:

The floorcoverings serve as a base color for all your merchandising efforts. When using carpet, a dark color tends to soak up available light. However, it also hides dirt and provides a rich backdrop to all your merchandise. In most cases, we specify a carpet in a medium tone with either a pattern or a mixed color element that complements other colors in the store. For instance, we have had a lot of fun with a commercial grade of carpet called Confetti by Harbinger Mills. The field color is available in blue, teal, black, lavender or mauve, and the rest of the floor appears to be strewn with multicolored confetti. The confetti colors can be pulled out into the fixtures, the ceiling banners, the slatwall, etc.

Vinyl, ceramic, or rubber tile also can be used to bring in a color element while wood floors can serve as a warm, neutral backdrop. The combination of multiple floor finishes and colors can be used both as a guide for store traffic and to emphasize distinct zones or merchandise areas within the store.

Ceilings are usually kept light in color to open the store up and because that's the way they come and it's just an added expense to paint them. If, however, the ceilings are very high or you are seeking more of an intimate, boutique or showroom look, the ceiling can be painted out a dark color and the lighting dropped to a height you are comfortable with. In essence, this makes the ceiling disappear and the merchandise on the floor and walls is emphasized.

Lighting fixtures will usually be finished in the same tones as the ceiling, particularly the track lamps. White ceiling—white light fixtures; dark ceiling—black fixtures. In most cases, unless you are shooting for a theatrical look, we try to make the light fixtures disappear. On the other hand, if the theme of the store calls for it, brass or chrome fixtures might be appropriate as accents.

The fixture colors give you the best opportunity to pull in interesting colors, finishes and detailing. Large fixtures, such as counters, cases and platforms, tend toward the neutral colors and should use punch colors for accent. The smaller display units, such as pedestals, risers and perimeter wall base units, also can pick up accent colors.

Graphics may be pulled in subtly, using colors that are a shadow of the field colors, or very boldly, with bright colors or interesting photos to attract attention.

Storefront materials usually are best kept in a neutral finish while the color of the store's front sign should jump out and grab customers. Sign colors will depend on store location. Strip center stores are off the street, so a bold color must be used just so people can see the sign. If you are in a mall, the colors can be a bit more subdued because the prospective customer is closer to the store and will be attracted as much, if not more, by the window display than by the sign.

The key with any color program is to remember that the walls, fixtures, ceilings, etc., are merely a backdrop to your merchandise. The colors should define and accentuate the environment of the store without detracting from the impact of the merchandise presentation. You don't want people walking in to your store and commenting on its color. They should be looking at the merchandise.

SUMMARY
By following this simple guideline for laying out your store, you should be able to create several workable diagrams for the store's design. After you have done so, pass the plan around and get some feedback. Show it to a designer or shopfitter and see if you are on the right track. It's much easier to make changes before the store is open than after the fact.

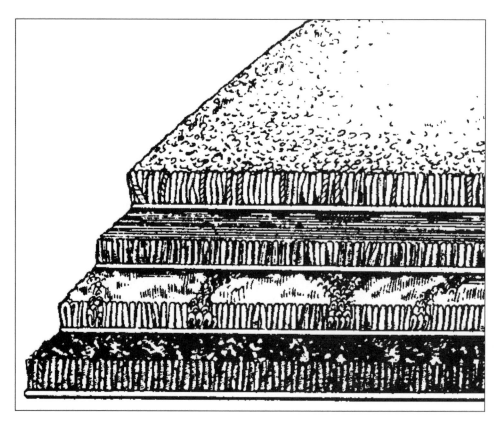

6 RETAIL FLOORCOVERINGS

Floorcoverings serve a dual purpose in a store. The first, of course, is to provide an attractive surface for your customers and employees to stand on. The second is to serve as a backdrop for your merchandise. In fact, the type of flooring you use will say much about the image you are trying to project for your store. In addition, by differentiating the type of flooring used in various store locations, a focal point can be gained for additional sales.

Selecting the floorcovering materials for a store is nothing like selecting floorcovering for a home. In a store, the traffic is greater, the maintenance higher and the visual aspect more critical. Cost, color and materials become important from an objective business point of view rather than a purely personal aesthetic.

Since the floor provides a continual backdrop for people and furniture, its finish and design can create an ambiance that is rich or poor, professional or utilitarian. Flooring can be designed to create an illusion of greater space or to define and accentuate particular areas. Design tricks used by store planners to promote traffic in particular areas might include:

• Using rubber, vinyl or ceramic tiles at the entryway and continuing the tiles through the store as a guide to lead your customers where you want them to go.

• Using the carpeting as the tile step-off to distinguish high-end merchandise areas such as clothing and accessories.

• Using different carpet styles or colors to differentiate specific sections of a store.

The flooring change stimulates customer interest and enhances product identification. The end result can mean heavier and more controlled traffic with a resulting increase in sales volume.

Initial flooring costs are very important, but long-term considerations also must be a factor in the flooring selection. In general, the resilient floors such as wood, stone and tile are quite expensive. Vinyl tile and sheet goods are less so. Carpet ranges from very inexpensive to quite expensive. However, along with the initial purchase and installation costs, the long-term maintenance costs must be factored into the buying equation.

CARPET
Long the favored material for most sporting goods and with good reason. Sound-absorbent, wear-resistant and available in an almost endless array of colors, finishes and prices. Purchase considerations include traffic flow, color and appearance, initial price and maintenance.

Traffic considerations have to do with the use and location of the area being covered. The following chart may clarify this.

Standard retail floorcovering plan. Tile at the entry, carpet everywhere else.

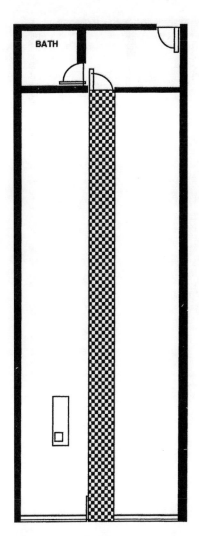

A little more creative. This design will pull the customer all the way through the store.

Area	Daily Traffic	Flooring Material
Private offices	light	commercial carpet
Retail space	heavy	heavy-duty nylon
Entry way	very heavy	heavy-duty nylon or resilient tile

The wear characteristics of carpeting have to be a major factor in its purchase. In most cases, you will get bored with a quality carpet before it wears out. However, carpet performance and longevity are tied to a combination of traffic patterns and fiber composition.

Wool is the standard by which all other carpet fibers are measured. Stain, crush and burn resistant, wool is hard to beat. The primary disadvantage is price. In most commercial installations, wool is almost prohibitively expensive and accounts for less than 1% of the contract flooring industry.

Nylon has become the predominant face fiber in most retail carpet installations. Latest-generation nylon flooring products provide excellent color, luster, soil resistance, wear characteristics and anti-static control. Pricing starts at about $12 per yard.

Acrylic approximates nylon in appearance, has good color and crush resistance, but has not done well in high-traffic areas due to low abrasion capabilities. This feature has been improved over the last few years and we are beginning to see more acrylic products in retail environments. Pricing starts at $6 per yard.

Polypropylene (Olefin) until recently was used heavily as a carpet backing and as indoor-outdoor carpeting. Stain, water, and sun-resistant, the major drawback to this fiber has been a limited color selection. However, recent advances in the finish and color of this product

This is a nice mix of wood and carpet. The plank entry creates interest while the carpet keeps the environment "warm". A good plan for clothing stores.

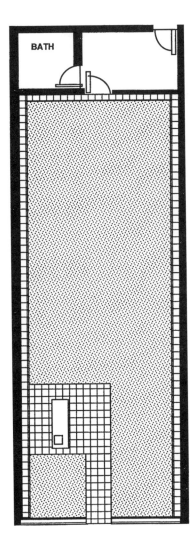

This plan is a little more expensive, but it's usually worth it. Tile or marble entry looks rich. Carpet acts as a field for merchandise presentation. The border attracts attention and defines the stores space.

have increased its specification and use. Pricing starts at $5 per yard.

Blends of nylon and acrylic can combine the characteristics of these two fibers to lower costs, increase performance or improve luster. Blended carpet fibers are becoming quite popular as an alternative for the buyer with a limited budget but a need for a high-quality flooring product. Pricing starts at $7 per yard.

Frankly, most commercial carpet dealers operate at a very slim margin, normally in the 20%-30% range vs. most residential flooring showrooms, which operate at 40% or better. If you acquire your floorcoverings through a commercial dealer, you should get exactly what you pay for. The higher the price, the more color and pattern selections you will have, along with the better wear and anti-stain characteristics.

Carpet Colors
Quite often, the carpet is the base point for a color scheme because it covers such a large area. Darker colors will mask soil, and nothing looks worse than stained carpet in a retail setting. Lighter colors show soiling and staining more readily than dark colors, while patterned colors hide stains better than solid colors.

Carpet Texture
The surface texture of the carpeting is important both from an aesthetic and a maintenance viewpoint.

• Level loop carpet is constructed of uncut loops of fiber tufted to the same height. Very sturdy.
• Multi-level loops have the carpet fibers tufted at two or more heights to add a sculpted look.
• Cut pile plush carpet has had the fibers sheared to produce a smooth loop combining the two textures.

Generally, the smoother the carpet, the easier it is to see stains. Loop carpets are better for hiding dirt and footprints. Cut pile shows both dirt and footprints a little more clearly, with a variance based on color and pattern.

Carpet Density

Carpet density has much to do with its acceptability as a flooring material in a commercial setting. Density of a carpet is expressed by its ounce weight and a formula is used to determine suitability for use.

$$Density = 36 \times face\ weight\ (oz./sq.\ yd) \div pile\ height$$

A figure of 3,000 to 4,000 is suitable for moderate traffic. A figure of 4,000 to 5,000 is suitable for high traffic. A figure of 5,000 or more is suitable for very high traffic.

For instance: A 24 oz. carpet with a 3/16-inch pile would have a density factor of 4608.
A 42 oz. carpet with a 1/4-inch pile would have a density factor of 6048.

A carpet that has a low price and a lower than suggested density formula may initially seem like a deal, but in the long run you may wind up making up the difference in price, in early replacement and excess maintenance costs.

Installation of carpeting is done using one of two methods: over a pad or glued directly to the subfloor. A quality grade of padding will preserve the appearance of the carpet and will add depth and comfort to the feel of the floor. Padding is more expensive than the direct-glue method and is usually inappropriate in large open areas where the carpeting has no anchor points other than the two ends. This will usually be the case in a retail store and we find the glue-down method is usually the appropriate choice.

Carpet tiles are the way of the future in retail design because of their flexibility in design and maintenance. Carpet tiles ease frequent floor layout changes and allow partial carpet replacement as high-traffic areas wear. However, the primary drawback to carpet tiles is price. In many cases the economics simply don't make sense.

Carpet prices are generally the most economical of any of the available floor options. Prices range from $5 to $45 per yard with $15 to $25 per yard the most common.

RESILIENT FLOORS

Resilient floorcoverings have been making somewhat of a comeback in the retail industry, primarily due to the development of new, low-maintenance products that provide a rich ambiance while maintaining all the benefits of hard floors: durability, stain resistance, color fastness and ease of maintenance. As these new types of floors develop, expect to see a greater acceptance of resilient floors as a substitute for carpeting in the retail environment.

Reinforced vinyl tiles are the most widely used of all resilient floorcoverings. Incredibly durable and stain-resistant, tiles are available in a wide variety of colors including the marbleized finish favored by most facility managers for its dirt-hiding abilities. Tiles are required to be buffed regularly, although with certain vinyl products, the need for waxing has been greatly reduced.

Vinyl comes in sheets or tiles and is a little more expensive than reinforced vinyl tiles. A soft material with a built-in luster, colors and surfaces are extensive and include realistic brick, wood and stone finishes. Because of the broad color spectrum available we frequently specify vinyl tiles for retail applications. However, due to its soft surface, we primarily use it as an accent to a more durable reinforced vinyl tile.

Rubber tiles are perhaps the most resilient of floors and have made a dramatic impact in recent years. Currently associated with high-tech, industrial-style rubber, it provides a very comfortable floor. Available in tiles and sheets, rubber needs to be washed regularly.

Wood floors were common up until the '50s, when carpeting started taking over the retail market. Wood floors are making a comeback, particularly in retail entryways and upscale active sport apparel shops. In fact, we now often specify wood plank maple floors to replicate basketball courts in sporting goods stores. These are available as a plank, strip or parquet, and unfinished or prefinished with a wood-impregnating acrylic that never needs waxing. Unfinished wood is

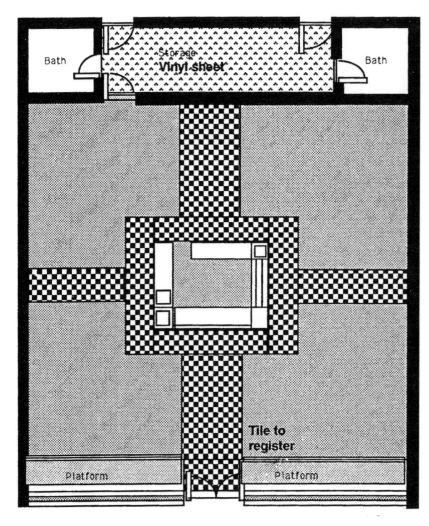

Larger, wider stores, can use floorcovering to define the merchandise space and attract customers throughout the store.

normally coated with a polyurethane finish, then waxed. The acrylic never needs waxing or other protective coatings.

Ceramic tiles are made of a baked clay and are both less expensive and easier to maintain than a masonry floor. Very versatile in terms of finish and color, tiles also are easy to lay in a variety of configurations. Tile is also a very low maintenance product.

Masonry is often a feature in upscale stores. Why? Because stone lasts forever. Marble, Travertine, onyx, granite and slate are all easy to maintain, rich and elegant in appearance, and visually stimulating. They also are all quite expensive, but are fun for special applications.

Installing resilient flooring is usually much more expensive than carpeting. Carpet runs $2 to $3 per yard to lay. Vinyl tile is $1 to $2 per foot; rubber the same. Ceramic tile and masonry can easily exceed $3 to $7 per foot depending on the complexity of the job.

SUMMARY

Choosing the proper floorcovering for your store takes both time and a careful analysis of your particular needs. It also requires a careful appraisal of both your long- and short-term budgets. A high maintenance floor or cheap carpet may save you some money initially but cost a fortune in upkeep or replacement over the long term.

Finally, remember that the profit margins in commercial carpeting are quite slim. If you are paying a very low price for goods that several other dealers have at a significantly higher price, something is wrong. You may be getting reduced ounce weight or seconds. In the commercial carpeting business, one gets exactly what one pays for.

QUICK FLOORING GUIDE

Retail Floorcovering Selections

Nylon Carpet

Nylon is the predominant face fiber in most retail carpet installations because it has excellent color, luster, soil resistance, wear characteristics and anti-static control. Pricing runs $12 to $30 per yard.

Olefin Carpet

Polypropylene (Olefin) until recently was used heavily as a carpet backing and as indoor-outdoor carpeting. Stain, water, and sun-resistant, the major drawback to this fiber has been a limited color selection. However, recent advances in the finish and color of this product have increased its specification and use. Pricing runs $6 to $12 per yard.

Nylons/Olefin Blends

Blends of nylon and Olefin combine the characteristics of the two fibers to lower costs, increase performance and improve luster. Quite popular as an alternative for the buyer with a limited budget but a need for a high-quality flooring product. Pricing runs $10 to $18 per yard.

Vinyl Tiles

Vinyl composition tiles are the most popular flooring choice and are particularly popular in discount and convenience stores. Indestructible and economical, the only drawback is upkeep. Buffing is a daily chore. Pricing runs 75¢ to $1.40 per foot.

Ceramic Tiles

Ceramic tiles offer the widest selection of color in both tile and grout of any floor material. Very wear resistant and easy to keep up. Pricing runs $2.30 to $5 per foot.

Rubber Tiles

Rubber tiles are perhaps the most resilient of floors and have made a dramatic impact in recent years. Currently associated with a high-tech, industrial style, rubber also provides a very comfortable floor. Available in tiles and sheets, rubber simply needs to be washed and buffed regularly. Pricing runs $2.75 to $4 per foot.

Wood Floors

Wood floors are making a comeback in retail, particularly plank styles vs. standard parquet. Upkeep is high as is pricing. Figure $4.50 to $6 per foot.

Granite and Marble Floors

Granite and marble floors are the most beautiful and resilient of all the hard surface flooring materials. Used in the finest shops these materials vary in price based on the stone used and its finish method. Minimum is $6 to $15 per foot.

Notes

Sometimes the best ceiling is no ceiling at all.

7 CEILINGS & SPACE FRAMES

You aren't selling ceilings, so it's usually not critical that you spend a lot of money creating something truly distinctive overhead. However, there are many cases where ceiling design considerations must be examined in light of the space, lighting or budget constraints placed on you by the landlord. In other instances, the overall theme or look of the store requires that some ceiling element be brought into play within the scope of the overall design. These elements might include:

• A non-ceiling; for example, a painted-out ceiling
• Banners
• Space frames and trussing systems

The use of any of these elements pulls the store out of the ordinary and can do much to enhance the overall feel of the space. Note that any of these elements may enhance the overall budget as well.

Ceilings can be used to distinguish merchandise presentation. The raising of a ceiling can provide the feeling of expansiveness and room required for the display of large objects such as sail boards, flying mannequins, scoreboards, etc. On the other hand, by lowering the ceiling in certain areas, a feeling of intimacy can be achieved. This technique works particularly well in sporting goods stores and apparel stores that sell a mix of large and small items.

Ceiling design will normally follow one of the following patterns:

Standard Drops
Dropped ceilings with 2 foot by 4 foot flat acoustic panels are the standard treatments you see time after time in countless retail establishments. They are the most economical way of installing a ceiling with lights and a heating and air conditioning system.

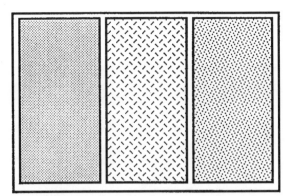

2'x4' ceiling tiles are still the most popular in retail environments even though pattern styles are very limited. Why? Price. 2'x4' tiles are cheap.

2'x2' ceiling panels are available in many patterns and finishes from textures to mirrors.

The ceiling grids support the lights, vents and the ceiling panels. The dropped ceiling panels act as the stop point for air treatment and circulation. In most cases, if you are going in to an existing store shell, this type of ceiling treatment already will be in place. Ninety percent of the time you should just accept them because in the scheme of things, upgrading the ceiling tends to be a very low budget priority.

2' x 2' Look-Alikes

If you want to change the look of a standard ceiling, the easiest and cheapest way to upgrade is to 2' x 2' look-alike panel as a replacement. Since the 2' x 2' panel has become the refined look in ceiling tiles, many manufacturers have started marketing a panel that is actually a 2' x 4' but has a detailed reveal that gives it the appearance of a 2' x 2' at a fraction of the price.

True 2' x 2's

The next upgrade would be to a true 2' x 2' panel, which would necessitate the installation of 2-foot runners as well as new ceiling panels. Keep in mind that current 2' x 2' panel styles can provide a variety of looks from contemporary to high-tech, from mirror reflective to glass block. Any of the above can easily be tied to the overall look of the store.

Aluminum Ceilings

This is another ceiling alternative and is available either as drop-in panels or a slat system that attaches to a ceiling grid. The aluminum panels are available in a wide variety of colors and finishes and can be an exciting addition to any store. Keep in mind that the price is quite a bit higher than most other types of ceiling treatments.

The Non-Ceiling

This is my favorite and we often use it in shops looking for a contemporary theme. We avoid the choice of ceiling tiles all together by opting to leave the ceiling out. Simply paint out what's up there with a dark color, drop your lights below the ceiling line, and forget about it. This type of look can sustain a high-tech theme that is difficult to achieve in any other manner.

The things to remember when following this path are:
1) Your air conditioning and heating bills will increase due to the larger volume of air that must now be dealt with vs. that under a dropped ceiling.
2) There will be the added expense of painting the ceiling and installing the lights.
3) You will probably have to work with a more expensive hard-surfaced vent duct rather than the flexible ducting used under a dropped ceiling because it is very difficult to get paint to adhere to flexible ducting.

Further you will often need to use a truss or space frame system (described below) to support the lighting when you remove the standard dropped ceiling.

Sculpted or Backlighted Ceilings

It is possible to build out the ceiling incorporating a sculpted or coffered look, or perhaps a backlighted

Skylights and banners can be quite dramatic.

faux skylight. This type of ceiling requires extensive framing and drywall and is one of those architectural elements that adds significantly to the drama of a store but pushes the budget up into the big leagues. If you can afford it and the overall store theme requires the look, you may want to incorporate this type of ceiling design.

Banners

Banners can add interest and contrast to the upper levels of a store, particularly if the ceiling is very high. Banners are usually fabricated from fire-treated nylon or canvas and are layered to create a multi-colored look. Sizes, heights and shapes will vary, as will the price. However, this is usually a very cost-effective way to lighten the feel of the shop and add interest and dimension to the ceiling. Further, banners can be screen-printed as a signing or display element on a permanent or seasonal basis. If you have an existing ceiling that is in bad shape or has exposed fluorescent lamps, banners can be a definite asset to the look of the store.

Space frames can add color and impact to any type of store.

Space Frames and Trussing Systems

Space frames and trusses are a relatively recent addition to the store planning lexicon. A trussing or frame system adds interest and creates a distinctive architectural element inside the store. Originally used as a method to visually lower the ceiling and to support lighting, space frames are now also used as a simple and exciting method of defining or identifying space, or as a support for signage or display.

Space frames will vary in price from $3 to $10 per square foot based on the frame product used, but they are worth the expense. We have used space frames in several sports stores to create an arena look and the results have been very popular.

Summary

If your budget is lean and the ceiling is in place, stick with it and add banners if necessary. If you have a few more dollars to work with, consider either 2' x 2' panels or a combination of panels and a space frame to really have some fun with the store.

Standard light track connections and lamp fixtures.

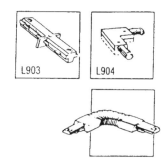

Universal
Accepts 50-150 watt bulb
Black or white

Continental
Accepts 50-150 watt bulb
Black Or White

Round Back Cylinder
Accepts 50-150 watt bulb
Black or white

HI Tech Swivel
Open Back, accepts 50-150
watt bulb. Black or white

Barn Doors
Directs light while adding
a theatrical look.

Mini Gimbel
High tech open back
Accepts 20-75 watt

8 LIGHTING

Nothing transforms the way a store looks like appropriate lighting. Proper display lights will punch up the excitement level on a sales floor by highlighting what's being sold. Not the carpet, the sales desks, the dressing rooms or anything else, just the merchandise. In fact, correct spot lighting can be used to pull customers through the store, stopping them at specific areas as they go. Most designers, even retail designers, know very little about the correct method of lighting a store simply because the technology has changed so much over the past few years.

In a nutshell, proper store lighting usually involves some combination of fluorescent ceiling fixtures, incandescent spot lights and low-voltage quartz lamps. The goal is to create enough light to sell goods and stimulate interest while still keeping your electric bill within reason. The key is not a lot of lights but the effective use of correct lamps. When lighting is designed into a store for both sales and display, not only will your product "pop," but your customer will also be comfortable and receptive.

Fluorescent Lighting
Fluorescent lamps are still best for general lighting in most stores. Unfortunately, the color rendition of standard fluorescent lamps is pretty dismal. Merchandise simply does not show its true colors under either "cool" or "warm" fluorescent lamps. Sylvania, along with several other manufacturers, has developed a line of fluorescent Designer Bulbs which provide a combination of high light output and color rendering performance that will make your merchandise really "sing." These lamps are designed for retail applications, use less power than a standard bulb, and can replace your existing fluorescents.

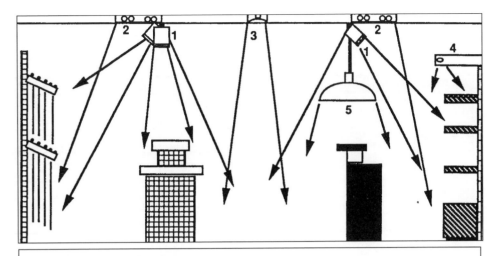

Lighting Legend

Lighting can be provided by several sources in a retail environment.
The diagram above details a possible lighting program for a sportswear store.

1) Track lighting
2) Fluorescent recessed lamps
3) Recessed incandescent lamps
4) Soffit strip lamps
5) Pendant hung Incandescent lamps

Most often fluorescent lamps are recess mounted in a dropped ceiling to create a flush ceiling surface. The major drawback of any fluorescent fixture is glare, so most fixtures are provided with a white plastic diffuser, which cuts the glare significantly.

Another problem is that light from fluorescent bulbs tends to be dispersed at ceiling level and never reaches merchandise below with sufficient intensity. Many retailers combat this problem by replacing the white diffusers with a chrome or brass-plated plastic egg crate diffuser that magnifies the light provided and redirects it toward the floor. The result is reduced glare at the ceiling and increased light on the merchandise. This is another added expense, but in many cases well worth the investment. Just make sure that the diffuser being used has a crate not less than 3 inches square, otherwise the light level may diminish more than it should.

Incandescent Lamps

Incandescent recessed or track lighting should be used for display and accent lighting. Most stores have ceilings at least 9 feet tall. At that height, light track fixtures should be large enough to accept par 38 spot bulbs so enough light will be thrown on your merchandise. Par 38 canisters will usually accept bulb wattages from 50-150 watts.

We often specify a 90-watt Sylvania Capsylyte Halogen bulb, which is the same size as a 150-watt spot bulb, has a higher light output and color rendering capability than a standard incandescent spot bulb, and uses significantly less power while generating less heat. The only drawback is price, which is about double that of a standard lamp. However, you will make that up in lower electric and air-conditioning bills over the long run.

Low-Voltage Quartz Lamps

Low-voltage quartz lamps are primarily used for high impact window and in-store displays where beam control is a must. These small quartz bulbs provide the highest color-rendition index of any bulb available, so merchandise looks better than under any other type of light. But the price is high.

Photometric Data

Legend:
F.C. – Foot Candles at beam center.
DIA – Beam Diameter in feet.
θ° – Beam Spread in degrees.
C.P. – Candle Power at beam center.

Lamp	JUNO Cat. No.	Type*	θ° Beam Spread	Max. C.P.	2' Distance		4' Distance		6' Distance		8' Distance	
					F.C.	Dia.	F.C	Dia.	F.C.	Dia.	F.C.	Dia.
xxW PAR30	T534-NS	NSP	11°	6,500	1,625	0.8	406	1.6	181	2.3	102	3.1
	T534-NF	NFL	28°	1,750	438	2.5	109	5.0	49	7.5	27	10.0
	—	FL	36°	1,100	275	2.5	69	5.0	31	7.5	17	10.0
75W PAR30	T535-NS	NSP	13°	10,500	2,625	0.9	656	1.8	292	2.8	164	3.7
	T535-NF	NFL	28°	3,000	750	2.5	188	5.0	83	7.5	41	10.0
	—	FL	36°	1,800	450	2.6	113	5.2	50	7.8	28	10.4
45W PAR38	—	NSP	7°	11,250	2,813	0.5	703	1.0	313	1.5	176	2.0
	—	SP	14°	5,000	1,250	1.0	313	2.0	139	2.0	78	4.0
	—	FL	28°	1,800	450	2.1	113	4.3	50	6.4	28	8.5
90W PAR38	—	NSP	7°	22,500	5,625	0.5	1,406	1.1	625	1.6	352	2.1
	—	SP	12°	13,000	3,250	0.9	813	1.7	361	2.6	203	3.4
	—	FL	30°	1,050	4,200	2.3	263	4.6	117	6.9	66	9.2

*KSP Narrow Spot: NFL–Narrow Flood, FL–Flood, SP–Spot

Photometric calculations are usually not skills a retailer needs to plan his own store,. However, we printed this chart just so you can get some idea of why bulb selection is so important. In most retail applications, tracklighting is used to create focal points within the store. To do this the foot candles of the track light bulb must exceed that of any daylight or existing fluorescent lamps. Further, the beam spread must be sufficient to spotlight what it is you are trying to display.

This chart shows the foot candles created by different bulbs at various distances from the merchandise it is hitting. Look at the lighting plan on this page to see how we used specific bulbs to crate an appropriate lighting plan.

Expect to pay $75 and up for a 75-watt low-voltage quartz track fixture and bulb vs. $35 for a standard track fixture with a 90-watt Capsylyte bulb. In most shops, other than for the display windows, we specify low-voltage lamps sparingly. Keep in mind that 50-watt or lower low-voltage bulbs cast very little light and won't make much of a dent in your general lighting program unless many lamps are used or lamps are quite close to the merchandise.

General Lighting Layouts

Several lighting plans are shown here. However, in most small stores the lighting layouts are fairly similar. Fluorescent lamps with diffusers are used to provide ambient lighting over the sales floor. Track lighting runs the perimeter of the store approximately 6 feet in from the walls and through the middle of the store on 8 to 10-foot centers to provide floor display focal lighting. Track cans are used every 3 to 4 feet with 75 to 90-watt Capsylyte bulbs. Low-voltage quartz lighting is often used in the front windows due to its color-rendition qualities and lean power requirements. Remember that window lamps are often left on after the shop closes.

In many sporting goods shops, we specify soffit lighting around the perimeter to attract attention and highlight wall merchandise. Fluorescents are the bulb of choice in this area punctuated by direct spots coming from the perimeter track.

Dressing Room Lights

Dressing rooms should not be lit from directly above the customer, particularly with fluorescent bulbs. Between the shadows cast and the poor color rendition, your customers can look quite wrinkled and faintly ghoulish. Try to use an incandescent light source over the dressing room mirror with the light directed toward the front of the customer. We often specify makeup-style cosmetic lights mounted directly over the fitting room mirrors. They provide great lighting and are little more fun than standard light fixtures.

"Leading with Lights"

How can you "lead" your customers with lighting? By creating display focal points that sparkle with light. Next time you're in a mall, see how many of the more sophisticated retailers have well-lit rear wall displays that are immediately visible from the front of the store.

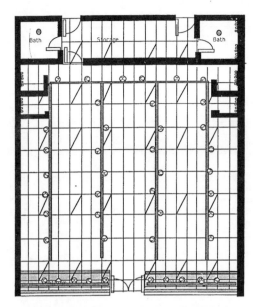

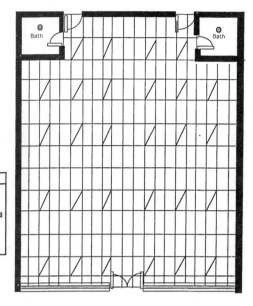

Standard lighting plan for a 2400 sq. ft gift or apparel shop in a strip center with existing lighting. Note the cosmetic lamps in the dressing rooms. If this were a gift shop we would specify some quartz track lamps to highlight high-end jewelry or crystal.

Existing lighting per landlord.

Light Legend

Cosmetic 20 watt lamps

90 watt capsylyte

Existing Flourescent lamps

These displays act like magnets pulling customers all the way to the rear of the store simply to see what's going on back there. Along the way, they are stopped by pools of light cast on specific merchandise displays.

Budget for your Lights
Don't skimp on lighting as a budget item. In retail, lighting has a faster payback than any other design element. If you must cut back on the lighting, rather than reducing lamps, try using a less expensive line of track fixtures, or different diffusers on the fluorescents. Replace the quartz lamps with standard incandescent units and hang the track yourself, simply using the electrician to hook up the power to the track ends. If you can find them, buy used track lights. They rarely wear out and tend to last for years. Used canisters will cost less than 25% of new.

Use a Lighting Designer
Finally, don't try to design the lighting layout on your own. Get experienced help. Ultimately, the extra sales volume and the savings in power usage will offset any additional lighting design expense. Further, most cities have energy ordinances and an energy calculation must be made with any permit application. You will not be able to do this on your own, although your electrician might be able to do it. In any event, I urge you to pay for a little help in this area.

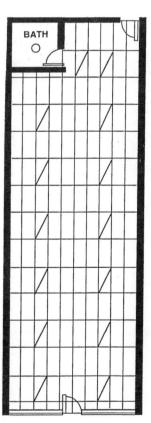

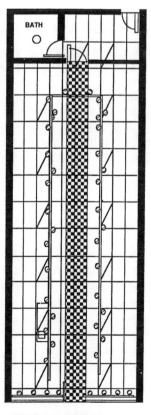

Standard lighting plan for a 1200 sq. ft gift or apparel shop in a strip center with existing lighting.

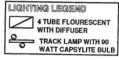

LIGHTING LEGEND

4 TUBE FLOURESCENT WITH DIFFUSER

TRACK LAMP WITH 90 WATT CAPSYLITE BULB

Don't be afraid to merchandise vertically in a small store.

9 MERCHANDISING, DISPLAY AND INTERIOR SIGNAGE

Often we design and build a beautiful store only to discover the owner does not have a clue how to best display the merchandise. Improperly merchandised goods will defuse the noblest attempts to create an interesting, profitable store. Apparel, hard goods, jewelry, sunglasses, balls, bats, you name it. If it's merchandised in a haphazard manner, the product will not sell as it should. Period.

Quite often this presentation chaos is the result of poor planning around the quantities and types of products the merchant intends to sell. Prior to entering the planning stages, work out an inventory list detailing the merchandise you plan to carry. If this is not done, you might wind up with either a store that looks empty or one that is bursting at the seams with a stockroom full of merchandise and no place to put it.

Go over your inventory requirements very carefully with your store planner and when the preliminary plan is complete, make sure that all the display and stocking requirements have been met with appropriate fixtures.

Establish a display style for your merchandising. This will vary depending upon your products. However, certain display concepts are common to all types of retail.

A store with all its merchandise at one level does not create interest or excitement. Plan to display your goods at different levels by using walls, pedestals and platforms to vary merchandise heights. Mid-floor merchandising levels should start at about 18 inches high and increase at 6-inch intervals to a maximum "reachable" height of 60 inches. Wall merchandising can go much higher and, in fact, many mall stores merchandise up to 12 feet high and salespeople retrieve products with hooks and ladders.

Experienced retailers will use a few merchandising tricks to increase sales. Display necessities in the rear of the store so customers have to pass impulse merchandise on the way back. (Ever wonder why milk and eggs are always at the back of the supermarket?) For instance a bike shop should have the bikes in the rear or on the side of the store and clothing toward the front and in the window. Group complementary or

Complete merchandising. Focal pionts are the shirts with ties on them. High points are the counter top racks. Stocking points are in the showcases.

Point of sale merchandising should be impulse oriented.

accessory items together such as socks near shoes, bats near balls, etc. Place high-margin, high-volume items at eye level so they will be seen and purchased. Place impulse items such as sunglass holders, sun block, key chains, etc., at the checkout stand for last-second purchases. Simple? Yes. Effective? Very much so.

DEVELOP A MERCHANSDISING SYSTEM

A straightforward program for merchandising virtually any product can follow a simple format. Recognize that every product from clothing to backboards can only be displayed in one of several styles, although these styles can and should be mixed.

Focal Points

First, plan to incorporate a series of specific, single-item or coordinated merchandise as focal points in attention-getting displays. These will include front window and in-store displays that are accentuated by spot lights. The focal points should start at the front of the store and march right on through to the back with stops every 6 to 7 feet. Make sure the focal point becomes just that by using narrow-beam spot lights to make the merchandise pop.

High Points

The next type of merchandising is a little less focal-ized and is called a high point. This type of display focuses on more than one object. For instance, a high point might include several shirts on a single shelf or perhaps a row of T-shirts on waterfalls utilizing a face-forward presentation. Perhaps a single 16-inch-square showcase on a 36-inch-high pedestal, accentuating 3 hand blown vases.

This type of presentation probably will constitute much of your display merchandising since it represents the best way to attract a great deal of interest to a wide variety of merchandise.

Stocking Points

A stocking point might include a stack of balls, or a run of magazines, or a grouping of pants or dresses hung on hangbar, shoulder-out rather than face-forward. The purpose of this type of merchandising is, of course, to get stock into the store and to create an impression of fullness. Many warehouse operations incorporate this type of merchandising because it seems to imply value simply though sheer quantity.

Point of Sale

The final type of merchandising is point-of-sale display. These are the items you incorporate into or around the front counter area to prompt impulse sales. The front counter may be the most profitable section of your entire store. Why? Because every customer who buys something from you needs to spend some time passing through that area. Many of our customers make more money at the check-out counter than anywhere else in the store. It's those impulse buys that really allow for volume sales with very high margins. Talk to the owner of a surf shop or sport store that incorporates a showcase as part of its checkout counter to hold sunglasses or wrist watches. Ask what percentage of total sales the wrap area produces. It's usually a real eye-opener.

Many of the front counters we specify are modular units that allow for expansion and a change in merchandising mix. For instance, a typical counter unit may be designed to hold only the cash register or point-of-sale computer, the credit card paraphernalia, a phone, a waste basket and a very small area for passing cash. Adjacent to the wrap is a showcase that is used as the primary spot to place merchandise being purchased. Anybody buying goods has to notice what is in that showcase.

Incorporated into that point-of-sale area might also be a tiered display unit that might hold key rings, pens with logos, or miscellaneous small impulse items. Pay careful attention to this area. It could return every dollar spent in multiples.

Levels of Display

All of your merchandising should occur at several different eye levels, again to prompt interest and traffic flow. The more levels of display you incorporate into your store's presentation, the greater the degree of interest you create. At least, as long as those levels are consistent and don't create a hodgepodge of merchandise that seems to lack any form, function or utility.

An analogy could be made to listening to a teacher giving a lecture. If the teacher seems devoid of emotion and simply delivers his speech in a monotone, you might fall asleep or leave before the lecture ends. If the speaker continually accentuates his speech with interesting anecdotes, and uses voice inflections to punctuate particular points, you will remain interested and listen willingly. Likewise, a store utilizing single-level merchandising without appropriate displays or

Linens sell best from a floor display. Just make sure you stock the merchandise shown close by. The same principle applies to any in-store display.

proper lighting may prove boring no matter how exciting the merchandise is. Let's deal with specific types of merchandise to clarify this concept.

Merchandising Clothing

The available merchandising options for clothing include shelving, binning, side-hanging, shoulder-out and face-forward waterfall presentation. This is punctuated by display focal points on forms or mannequins.

In most stores, the initial merchandising presentation starts in the front window with a dramatic display and continues into the store with focal points primarily along the wall perimeters. The focal points might include mannequins, forms, scarecrow displays or backlighted photos of models wearing the type of clothing you sell. Or, perhaps action shots relating to the specialty equipment you carry (surf, sail, dive).

The high points would include clothing on presentation racks and waterfalls. These should vary in height and style. Waterfalls should be both slanted and straight-out to again create interest and to differentiate product. Folded apparel on tier tables also creates a high point of interest.

Stock points will feature clothing displayed shoulder-out on hangbar or folded into bins, on pegs or in masses (socks, hosiery, belts).

Make sure the fixture system you use gives you the flexibility to merchandise either as a high point or a stock point. Why? Because high pointing allows you to

make the store look very full with very little merchandise. It is possible to fill up a 4 by 8-foot wall section with four waterfalls holding 24 garments or two 48-inch sections of hangbar requiring 100 garments to fill out. With flexible merchandising, you can switch from waterfalls to hangbar as your stocking and display requirements dictate. You don't want your store to look empty. Ever.

Merchandising Gifts

Gift merchandising is somewhat different than clothing presentation. The heights used are a little lower simply because it hurts more to have a glass vase fall on your head than it does a Calvin Klein jersey. Most merchandising is done on a flat surface or a specialty display of some sort.

The focal point concept is again pulled into play with interesting windows and staggered displays running through the store to the back walls. Narrow-beam spot

Legs always attract attention. A good combination of focal points strengthening the sale of bread and butter merchandise.

lights may have to be used because the product is relatively small compared to apparel. More focal points should be placed mid-salesfloor atop pedestals or risers because the mass of the walls will dwarf most gift focal displays. Even on the sales floor, the size of your products can be so small that a display pedestal will be necessary to attract additional attention. Focal point lighting in gift shops usually goes to 50 to 75-watt low-voltage quartz lights.

High points might include grouped objects in showcases, or short rows of similar merchandise (crystal, mugs, toys, plush) on shelves or atop pedestals. Most rows should be broken up with multi-level plastic risers to add dimension to the display. Lighting usually will be medium spots.

Stock points include masses of product. Check how Pier One carefully stacks stem glasses or the Pottery Barn groups mugs, or IKEA stacks folded chairs, or Toys R Us shelves models cars and planes. All are examples of stock points. These areas usually will be lit with the ambient lighting provided by the fluorescent lamps rather than the spots being used on focal and high points.

A word about showcases. Anything placed under glass is perceived to have value. If you are trying to create a high-end look either throughout your store or in specific spots, utilize showcases extensively. Just make sure they are well-lit, otherwise no one will be able to see what is for sale inside of them.

Other Types of Stores
The same merchandising formulas will work whether you are selling auto parts, food, toys or sunglasses. Attract attention with focal points, interest with high points and a sense of depth of merchandise with stock pointing. Utilize the walls and floor fixtures to create differentiation in display heights.

Most importantly, don't assume that just because your product is a little more mundane than clothing, jewelry or artwork, that you don't need to worry about display. Over the last 12 months, our design department has worked on new showrooms for air conditioning supply warehouses, plumbing stores, paint shops, motorcycle dealerships, drugstores and even car washes. Every retailer has to be concerned about both the competition and appropriate display. How else will your customer know what you have to sell? Further, why else

Windows attract customers like nothing else will. If you don't know how to dress your windows correctly, find someone who can.

will they buy from you rather than the shop down the street?

If you don't know how to merchandise your products, talk to other merchants who seem to be doing a good job. Find out who helps them. In many cases, a competent window trimmer also can become involved with the initial merchandising format. In most cases, he or she will have the necessary experience to set up your store effectively. They also can help you set up a basic merchandising program, train your staff and support the program on a monthly basis.

One final note on merchandising. Quite often, display accessories such as bags, size dividers, hangers, steamers and even price tags are not ordered till the last minute. At the time you need these items most, the fixture supplier may be out of stock and your merchandise winds up sitting in a box. Order early.

Window Display
Window display is the most important part of store merchandising because, in many cases, it is the first contact the customer will have with your store and his reason for entering in the first place. The style of

window display will vary depending upon the merchandise being presented.

For most clothing stores, full-size mannequins are still the best method of showing apparel. However, it is all too easy to buy cheap-looking mannequins with stilted poses. If you plan on using mannequins, buy only the best. Most mannequin manufacturers have showrooms in New York and Los Angeles and reps in major cities. Expect to pay $600 to $800 per mannequin plus freight and expect a six to eight week delivery period. If this is a little outside your budget, try buying used mannequins from a dealer. Have your window trimmer help with selection and expect to pay about $350 each.

If your budget is even leaner or you don't like the look of full-sized mannequins, try steel tube forms or flat foam forms, which are designed to show off clothing at a very reasonable price. Or, don't use body forms at all and simply "fly" clothing from the ceiling by tying to a grid hung horizontally over the window.

Gift shops and other retailers can use a series of raised wood or laminate pedestals to display product at different levels in the front windows. Props also can be

Wide store fronts act as display windows without the glass. Make sure you tell a story in the entry.

used to support gift items. Try crates, bikes, wheels, windows, weird stuff, anything that you don't sell, that looks fun, that helps attract interest while either supporting product or adding to the display window's theme.

In any event, plan to maximize your window display opportunities. Don't just throw your products into the window with little rhyme or reason. Pick a theme around the season, a holiday, a current event, a location. One of my clients put a convertible car in his window, complete with mannequins, surfboards and hanging dice balls. The display made the evening news.

My company sells Christmas displays around October of each year. Several seasons ago, we put a Santa in our front widows clad only in boxer shorts, holding a sign that said, "Don't get caught with your pants down, shop for X-mas displays now." We made the front page of the daily newspaper.

Hire a window trimmer to create your window displays. Expect to pay $75 to $150 per month for the trimmer plus the cost of props. You can find a creative window trimmer the same way you can find a designer.

Ask around. Be sure to clarify the cost of the window trimming labor vs. the cost of props. Find out if the trimmer has props to rent. Create a display schedule with the trimmer and invest some time and energy into planning your displays. Your efforts will provide immediate gratification in both sales and customer recognition.

Interior Display

Many of the same props and display ideas discussed for window display can also be used in the store if you have, or make the room. In any department store you will see several displays for each department that provide a clear impression of what is for sale in that area. These displays serve as focal points generating interest and traffic flow. In a small store you might not have room for additional mannequins or extensive props, but additional focalized display merchandising will add a great deal of interest within the store and the suggestive selling should add to overall sales volume.

I was recently in a Hobie surfboard shop in Maui, Hawaii, that had an extensive historic surfboard collection mounted around the perimeter of the store at the

You can't miss this boy's section. The style and size of the lettrs add to the fun in the store.

8-foot level. The store had as many people in it looking at the board collection as they did at bikinis. But all those lookers bought merchandise.

Interior Signage
Signs can tell your products' story, keep customers in the store longer, guide them from display to display, and act as a silent salespeople. Effective signs can free up your floor sales staff to wait on customers whose questions have not been answered by the signs. Look at the crowds in The Sharper Image and Brookstone stores. The signs hold them in the store more than the merchandise.

Vendor logo banners and point-of-purchase displays do much to add interest to your store's overall look. Don't, however, forget to create signs that talk about sales, special products, promotions, etc.

Photo blowups and props also can do much to add to the store's theme or merchandising presentation. Large, changeable, backlighted photo transparencies have become very popular for merchandise presentation both in larger shops such as The Gap and Espirit as well as many smaller, more progressive

stores that solicit stock artwork and photos from their vendors.

Ideally, create an in-house, logoed sign program with your designer that ties in with the rest of the store's identity. This could be in the form of preprinted sign card that receives additional handwritten or printed information as needed.

Other signage efforts can be made using individual plastic, foam or ceramic letters in a variety of fonts, colors and sizes, all available from your display distributor. We also work closely with local sign shops that have access to computers that cut out vinyl letters for mounting to sign boards, walls, windows or soffits.

In summary, use signage to supplement and enhance your merchandising program. Don't create a hodge-podge of hand-lettered signs. Pick a style, use professional sign makers and maintain consistency .

Video
Video can create more excitement in your store than any single display item. The mechanics are quite simple. You can rent or buy individual monitors and place them throughout the store. Prices will range from $350 to$650 per monitor. These can be set up to run individually or in sync. You can buy banks of monitors that may stretch 4 wide by 4 high and that present both individual pictures and 4 by 4 montages to create an unmatched visual impact. These run about $42,000 plus freight and installation. That's why you tend to see banks of monitors in the larger stores.

Play with the video if you can. Put it in the floor with glass over the top of it, behind a basketball backboard, or on top of a skater's head. Get creative, buy great video tapes, and keep the monitors on all the time. Nobody likes to see a blank screen.

Summary
The key to a great-looking store is great merchandising. You can fill a store with great fixtures, colors, carpets and lights and immediately trash the store with lousy display. On the other hand a talented merchandiser can make an empty square box "sing." The least expensive thing you can do to upgrade your new or existing sore is to have it merchandised correctly. Use the ideas in this book and hire some talented help.

10 WALL AND FLOOR FIXTURES

Fixture systems are usually either off-the-shelf products supplied by store fixture distributors and manufacturers, or custom units supplied by local craftsmen. Major department stores and chain stores quite often use custom fixtures that may have been designed exclusively for their firm while smaller retailers will usually buy their equipment from mail order fixture catalogs or local distributor showrooms.

For most merchants, custom fixtures are economically not only unfeasible but may amount to overkill. More apparel won't be sold because a clothing rack has bleached wood uprights and Lucite display arms rather than standard chrome fittings. Why spend $500 for a fancy display fixture when a $200 unit will tell the same story? We do, however, encourage our clients to choose custom fixtures if they fit the overall theme of the store as well as their merchandising needs and budget. For example a surf shop might use surfboards cut in two lengthwise and mounted to the wall as shelving for shirts and pants. Or a shop with a country motif might use period oak or mahogany amoirs to stock and display merchandise. A sporting goods store could use basketball rims to act as support for glass display shelves.

Keep in mind that what is being sold is what's on the fixture, not the fixture itself. A fixture serves merely as a backdrop to the merchandise. Be that as it may, the fixture's style should not clash with that of the store. Why open a high-end women's active clothing boutique if you are going to merchandise the dresses on round chrome racks? The presentation winds up detracting from the merchandise rather than highlighting it.

In choosing a fixture system, look and versatility must be balanced with cost. If you are building a single store on a relatively small budget, do not expect to use many custom fixtures. Instead, concentrate on some combination of "off the shelf" equipment that suits your particular needs at a moderate cost. Combine fixtures that are so specialized they are only suitable for a particular application within the store's specialty requirements (such as a hosiery bin), or versatile enough to allow for multiple presentation postures (such as a grid pin-

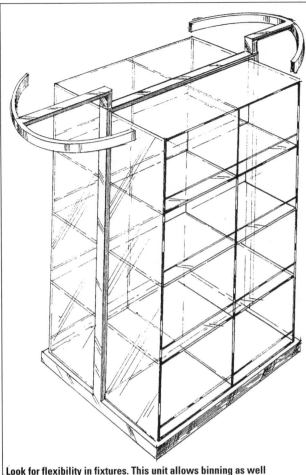

Look for flexibility in fixtures. This unit allows binning as well as hanging

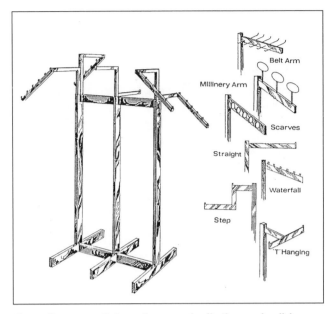

Custom fixtures aren't always the answer in effective merchandising

wheel, a slatwall tower or display pedestals). If you don't have the money to plug in custom fixtures, add interest to your equipment with paint and laminate colors that have little effect on pricing.

Fixture systems can be mixed quite effectively. For instance, a sports store might utilize wall fixtures that include a combination of recessed standards, slatwall and grids. Floor fixtures would be comprised of two- and four-way racks, glass bins, and tier tables. This combination of display equipment will allow you to manipulate the budget, create interest in various sections within the store and to differentiate merchandise presentation.

Keep in mind that there is not a single best way of presenting your merchandise. Your store's fixture plan should take into account your merchandising format and your budget. The combination of the two will lead you to your store's most appropriate fixture layout.

Most fixture systems are used either for wall display or for floor merchandising. Some can be used for both.

For example, grids can be used mounted to a wall or freestanding as gondolas. Slatwall panels can be used in much the same manner.

WALL FIXTURES

Wall display should emphasize merchandise presentation rather than merchandise stocking. If your store has been well-planned, much of the perimeter of the store will be visible from the front door. This means the displays on the walls will be instrumental in creating traffic flow throughout the store. If the wall fixtures do not provide the flexibility required to effectively merchandise your products, traffic circulation will suffer as will sales. System-oriented equipment such as slatwall, gridwall, or standards and brackets, offer the opportunity to change the look of your store by merely changing around a few fixture accessories. Many custom fixtures don't afford the same luxury.

The systems described here are primarily off-the-shelf units that can be purchased through your fixture dealer. Most can also be used in conjunction with custom

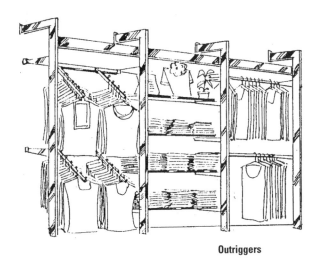

Outriggers

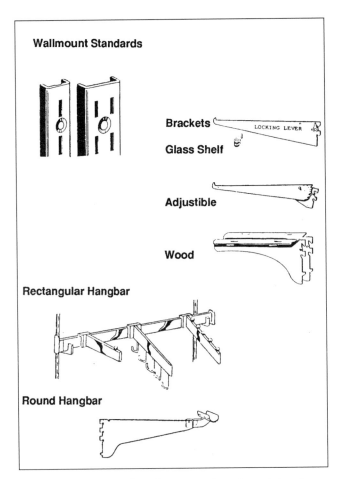

Wallmount Standards

Brackets
Glass Shelf

Adjustible

Wood

Rectangular Hangbar

Round Hangbar

Standard and brackets will service most retail requirements from hang-bar to shelving.

equipment to create a "special" look that is unique to your store.

Standards and Brackets

Wall-mounted slotted standards are still the most popular wall fixturing system available, and with good reason. Economical, strong, easy to obtain and quite versatile, standards are the backbone of many stores' merchandise presentation.

Standards either wall-mount to studs or are recessed into the wall, leaving only a slot showing that is the thickness of the required brackets. Wall-mounted standards can be put in place over any level wall surface, while recessed standards will only fit behind the wall surface. Both types accept brackets that will allow the merchant to display virtually any type of product from gifts to clothing.

Shelf brackets are available in depths of 6 to 25 inches and allow either wood, metal or glass shelves to be used. Adjustable brackets also are available that allow shelves to slant up or down.

Round hangbar brackets support clothing hangrod for shoulder-out merchandising of clothing. Rectangular brackets support rectangular hangbar, which can be used for either shoulder-out display or a waterfall, face-forward presentation (see picture).

Standards are usually attached to the wall with wood screws every 24, 32 or 48 inches. We rarely use 48-inch centers for shelving because most shelves will sag with that size span. The most common centering is 32 inches.

Outriggers and Light Soffits

These are simply a derivative of wall-mounted standard and bracket. Usually fabricated from wood or

metal with slotted standard backs facing the wall, outriggers provide flexibility while adding a slightly more expensive, refined look to the wall display. The uprights tend to frame the merchandise, creating specific areas within the wall expanse. In many cases, we use outriggers simply to define a particular area within the store space.

Outriggers are often used to support lighted soffits. Again, this can greatly add to the refined look of the store, in most cases at very little added expense. A soffit strip is simply mounted to the face of the outriggers and a lamp attached to the backside of the soffit. The light created attracts immediate attention to the area involved and the face of the soffit provides additional opportunities for signage.

One additional benefit occurs when dealing with either large window areas or unstable walls. The outrigger pulls the bearing weight off the face of the wall, allowing an attaching point at the floor and ceiling (or just above the window). This type of fixture program can be a real merchandising solution for stores in historical sites with adobe or brick walls, and to hotels or hospital shops that have lots of windows and little wall space.

Gridwall and Slatwall

Gridwall and slatwall are two relatively new merchandising systems being used to display merchandise of all types. Gridwall is fabricated from 1/4-inch wire welded into 2 foot- by 6-, 7-, or 8-foot-high grids in a variety of colors and finishes. The grids are either attached to the store's walls or configured into tables, gondolas, pinwheels or columns to provide a display platform.

Slatwall is a wood system in which 4-foot high by 8-foot wide medium-density fiberboard is covered with a plastic laminate or a wood finish and channels are routed into the surface. The finished panels are then secured to the wall or are fabricated into display towers or gondolas.

Slatwall is available with metal, plastic or laminate inserts that slide into the routed channel for decoration or additional support. The laminate strip is merely decorative and is used as a color contrast to the slatwall face color. The plastic or metal insert is a method of strengthening the panel for additional merchandise support.

Both systems incorporate metal and plastic accessories that attach at any given spot on the grid or panel and effectively display all types of products. Gridwall and slatwall offer tremendous versatility and a contemporary look at a relatively low cost.

Gridwall is particularly well-suited to the active sports industry due to the weight of much of the clothing and equipment. Grids can hold loads of leathers, wetsuits, tires, accessories, clothing, and more, without strain.

Slatwall offers a slightly more refined look with a much greater choice of available colors. Finishes available include plastic laminates from Formica, Nevamar, Laminart and Wilsonart. This color flexibility lets you color coordinate the store with the carpet, walls, counters and other color details.

Pegboard

Pegboard gondolas are still very popular in sporting goods and hardware stores and with good reason. Pegboard gondolas with steel shelves are perfect for stocking bulk merchandise. Further, manufacturers produce display accessories for pegboard to support all types of merchandise, from golf clubs to fishing poles.

Gridwall

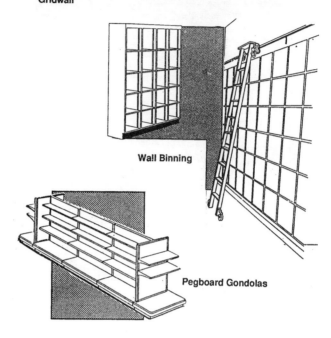

Wall Binning

Pegboard Gondolas

Use pegboard gondolas in stores that require mass merchandising. The look is dated, so if budget allows use slatwall back panels or at least color-coordinated pegboard backs.

Base Cabinets

We often use 18 to 24-inch-high by 18 to 20-inch-deep base cabinets as the starting point for our wall displays in many shops. These bases add a richness to the store that slatwall and shelves running to the floor never will. Base cabinets also can provide storage in tight quarters.

Wall Binning

Usually glass, wire or wood bins are used to merchandise folded apparel. Set atop base cabinets, these may extend up as high as 10 feet with rolling ladder access.

FLOOR FIXTURES

Floor fixtures pull customers through the store in stages (rack to rack, shelf to shelf). The floor displays must be interesting enough to keep that momentum

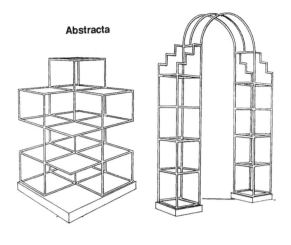

Abstracta

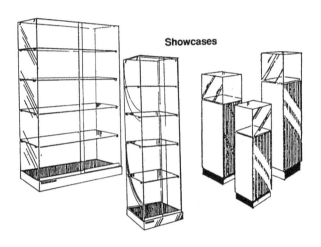

Showcases

going to the rear of the store. The key is a combination of product and merchandising. If the product is displayed correctly on the floor fixture, the customer will make a decision to stop and take a look. If the fixture does not allow for adequate merchandising opportunities, it may be impossible to display your products effectively. For example a round rack only shows the side of a garment, not the front. Who would be attracted to a roomful of the sides of garments? (Unless you are a discount operation where that look might fit the theme.) Try to utilize floor fixtures that allow for multiple merchandising methods.

As with the wall fixtures, the systems described here are primarily off-the-shelf units that can be purchased through your local shopfitter or mail order catalog. Most can also be used in conjunction with custom equipment to economically create special fixtures that don't cost a fortune.

Abstracta

For a contemporary or high-tech accessory look, try Abstracta shelving units fabricated from chrome, brass or painted metal tubes with glass shelves. Off-the-shelf from a fixture supplier, these units come in virtually

any size or configuration and are perfect for showing specialty sport accessories. The tubing is only half an inch in diameter so it does not detract from the merchandise and in fact imparts a light "airy" feeling to the presentation.

Showcases

Showcases not only display product, they identify that merchandise that has enough value to be put behind locked doors. Be certain your cases imply value. In other words, buy quality showcases, light them, use mirrored doors and color-coordinate the bases with the rest of the showroom. Showcases come in virtually any size or finish and can be be used on the sales floor or up against the walls of the store.

Showcases are either custom-made in a local shop, factory-made domestically or imported, usually from Italy. The custom case will always be the most interesting and elegant (and expensive) as long as your cabinet shop understands how to build it and is familiar with glass and lighting. Available domestic cases usually are built with metal extrusions to hold the glass, wood and doors in places and come with a series of options. These options include mirror doors, locks, lights, custom finishes and drawers. The nice thing about these cases is the price usually will be right.

Italian manufacturers started a big push to get their showcases into the U.S. several years ago and that effort has met with a great deal of success. The cases are all glass and held together with unobtrusive metal clips. These cases provide a lot of style for the price and many retailers use them extensively.

Platforms and Pedestals

We seem to specify multiple Formica platforms and pedestals for virtually every shop we are involved with. Normally, 14 to 24 inches square and rising in height from 18 to 42 inches in 6-inch increments, these fixtures are perfect for focal and high-point merchandising. In some cases, we add a revolving top or showcase to the pedestal, depending upon the specific display requirements.

Metal Clothing Racks

Use apparel racks to display clothing. You don't need anything fancy. Just stick with standard two-way and four-way presentation racks placed strategically on the sales floor.

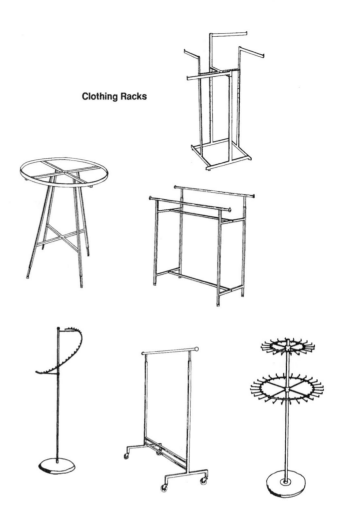

Clothing Racks

Colored racks have been making a comeback in many areas, but I urge caution in buying anything other than white or black racks. As styles change, those red four-way racks are going to clash a bit with your pastel spring lines.

Try to avoid round racks simply because they only show the sides of the clothing, not the front. It's hard to sell shoulders. Round racks are excellent for displaying promotional goods or as sale racks.

If you need to stock up on merchandise, do so on hangbar along the lower walls of the store with face-forward waterfalls above rather than with round or double-bar racks. If stock is low, you can replace the lower hangbar with more waterfalls so the store won't look empty. You can't easily replace round racks with four-ways at a moment's notice to achieve the same objective.

Tier Tables

Folding clothing has become a very popular method of merchandise presentation over the past few years and the tier table has taken on increased importance as a merchandising tool. Manufactured from wood or metal, these tables provide another dimension for your display efforts. Use them in wide open areas of the sales floor. Don't tier below 24 inches or above 48 inches, and be prepared to spend a lot of time keeping the garments on the table neat.

Tempered Glass or Wire Display Units

Tempered glass bins often are used to store shirts, sweaters, gloves and other apparel. We put bins on a color-coordinated base and use standard 10 by 10 by 16-inch-deep cubes for shirts and sweats. Bins also are available in wire mesh for a slightly more "tech" look.

Slatwall and Gridwall

Slatwall and gridwall panels can be configured in to gondolas, towers, "H" units, "Z" units and other interesting floor displays that are both versatile and attractive. Gridwall in particular can create a flexible display fixture at a very moderate price. Many active sports and accessory shops use grids extensively to fabricate display racks for the display a wide variety of products. See the merchandising section of this book for further discussion on this.

Pegboard Gondolas

These also may be used as floor fixtures for all the same reasons they are used along the walls. Able to support loads of merchandise and very flexible, these are the fixture of choice in many stores.

VENDOR DISPLAYS

In recent years, many manufacturers have grown concerned about the presentation of their products in the retail environment. Therefore, they have attempted to control the merchandising by supplying merchants with low-cost point-of-sale fixtures that provide appropriate presentation and signage. Try to work with these displays sparingly and only if they fit within your total store merchandising package. Many times I have seen a carefully color-coordinated store skewered by a hodgepodge of off-color vendor racks. If you like the product, buy it. If the vendor rack that comes with the product doesn't fit into your stores decor, don't use it.

OTHER FIXTURE SYSTEMS

Many other display systems are available and in most cases, an off-the-shelf system will look and work better at a substantially lower price than a custom system. Your fixture supplier should have pictures and

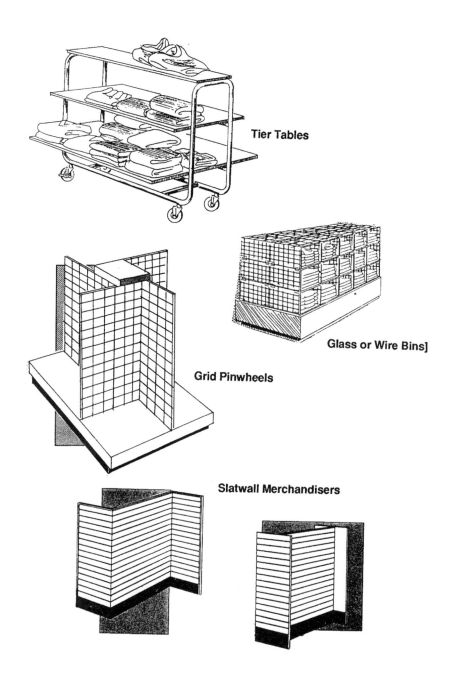

Tier Tables

Glass or Wire Bins]

Grid Pinwheels

Slatwall Merchandisers

brochures on a wide range of products that will work for your particular operation. Additionally, he should have access to cabinet makers accustomed to building quality retail store fixtures for any special work that may need to be done.

BUYING EQUIPMENT

New store equipment is usually acquired through the manufacturer, from a local distributor or via a mail-order catalog. In many cases, the fixtures you see in a distributor's showroom or catalog are only available through that network and manufacturers will not deal with you directly.

On the other hand, the wonderful mannequins, displays and fixtures you see in department stores are usually only supplied through the manufacturer and you will need to order directly. If you are close to a major metropolitan area, the factory might have a local rep; otherwise you will have to order though their catalog. Most manufacturers have showrooms in L.A. or New York, so visiting them might be a step to take if you are making a significant investment.

A national visual merchandising and display show is held in New York every May and December and you can familiarize yourself with many of the available fixture and display systems by attending the show. It is called "the NADI show" for National Association of Display Industries. Another large fixture show is held in Chicago in the spring and is called appropriately, The Store Fixturing Show.

Most fixture distributors buy from the same sources, so the product is usually the same, although the prices may not be. National catalog prices usually will be lower than your local distributor's simply due to economies of scale. National firms buy in larger quantities, so their first price is lower and that cost saving is passed on to the customer.

Of course, the downside to dealing with a mail-order firm in Chicago or New York is the freight, service and convenience factor. I suggest that before you order any new merchandise, you comparison-shop the national catalogs, then sit down with the local distributor to see what you can work out on the pricing.

In particular, if you are building a store with items that are not right off the shelf such as custom counters, storefronts, lighting, flooring, etc., you will need local professionals who understand the building codes and can deal with problems on a day-to-day basis. Further, if you need to have your store equipment set up or installed, a local distributor will be in a better position to perform those services for you than someone who is out of the area.

Used Equipment

Used fixtures can be a real find, and most distributors do some dealing in used equipment. The good news is, of course, price, price and price. The bad news is that most used equipment looks it. Chipped, bent, rusty or simply abused, it is very difficult to find a quality used product. You can't afford to have a new store filled with shoddy-looking equipment. It will ruin any notions the customers have about the quality of your merchandise.

What can you buy that usually is in good shape or is salvageable? Racks, grids, showcases, mannequins, glass bins and lighting. Any cabinet work has to be looked at very closely and used carpet is usually too beat to use. I advise you to try to find used goods but

don't let the potential savings stand in the way of opening your store on time or creating a quality look.

Terms

Some fixture suppliers will give terms and some won't. If your firm is Dunn and Bradstreet listed and your credit checks out, many firms will extend credit for 30 days. If you are relatively new in business the chances of getting credit are slim to none. Don't expect to get great prices and great terms. For most seasoned suppliers, the refrain runs, "Your price, my terms. Your terms, my price."

Leasing Equipment

Very few of my customers lease their store equipment, although it has always seemed like a good idea to me. Why tie up your cash in fixtures when you can use it to buy inventory that can be turned at a keystone several times a year? Further, if your business is a corporation, you could buy the equipment personally and lease it to your corporation preserving the depreciation for your own tax needs.

There is a correlation between money spent on store design and equipment, and the store's success. If a lease will let you invest a little more in the "look" of the store, it may be an investment that has a very substantial return. Leasing has more to do with taxes than it does with store design, so I won't dwell on it. However, I encourage you to discuss leasing with your accountant as a viable method of financing your store's equipment.

Equipment and Designers

One final note on specifying fixtures. As discussed early in this book, most designers and architects are unfamiliar with retail equipment. Don't have them spend your money reinventing the wheel. Either give them some idea of the equipment you want to incorporate into your store or call in a store fixture consultant early in the design process.

11 EXISTING STORE EVALUATION

A store's physical systems have to be maintained on a regular basis or the store will quickly start to look shoddy. Likewise, the merchandise in the store always must be displayed appropriately or the customer either won't be able to find a product or sense its value. The successful merchant is consistent in both store maintenance and merchandising.

I have seen many merchants build a beautiful store and within six months (or less) become complacent or simply lazy and let the store's merchandising and upkeep go to pot. Some retailers have been in business for so many years that they can no longer see what a mess their store really is. The result of this lack of consistency is a loss of sales. But the condition can be reversed.

Much of this book appears to be geared toward the creation of new retail spaces. However, the same merchandising and design principles that pertain to new stores also are applicable for existing stores. The following is a questionnaire for existing merchants to use in evaluating the look of their store. By using this checklist on a consistent basis, you should be able to notice any shortcomings your store has and respond to them.

After you have reviewed this checklist and have decided to remodel or at least revitalize your store, what should you do first? Based purely on a cost/benefit analysis, I suggest you take these steps in this order:

1) Clean the store inside and out.
2) Retain a skilled, part-time window trimmer and instore merchandiser who can help you with new display ideas.
3) Re-merchandise to create points of interest in your products.
4) Rearrange the fixtures and equipment to encourage traffic flow.
5) Make sure the front window displays are fun, exciting and interesting.
6) Change any inappropriate light bulbs.
7) Repaint the store inside and out if required.
8) Add some focal-point lighting.
9) If the floorcoverings are stained or worn, replace them with the best product you can afford.
10) Upgrade your store fixtures and signage.

The first six steps will require a very limited investment of money. The next four steps could cost a small fortune. I suggest that once you have cleaned the store and re-merchandised, figure out what you want to budget for upgrading the store. Then hire a store designer on an hourly basis to work on what you should do next and what it's going to cost you.

EXISTING STORE CHECKLIST

A) Storefront
    1) Are the windows clean and intact and is the front sidewalk well-swept?
    2) Does the storefront paint look faded or dull? Is it time for a repaint?

B) Front Sign
    1) Is the sign in one piece with the letters all in place?
    2) Is the sign well-lit?
    3) Can prospective customers look at your sign and tell exactly what it is you sell?

C) Front Display Windows
    1) Are your front window displays effective?
    2) Have they been changed in the last four weeks?
    3) Are your window props or displays in reasonable shape? Do the mannequins have stilted poses? Are they all in one piece or are fingers broken and wigs askew?
    4) Are the windows deep enough to tell an effective story?

D) Floorcoverings
    1) Does the floor look stained or worn?
    2) Is the carpeting lying flat, freshly vacuumed and clean?
    3) Do you need a resilient floorcovering (tile, rubber, wood) at the entryway to reduce wear?

E) Ceiling
    1) Are any ceiling tiles missing or stained?
    2) Are the vent grills dirty and stained?
    3) Does the ceiling need paint?
    4) Are there any ceiling details that attract unwanted attention?

F) Lighting
    1) Does your existing lighting system provide adequate light to all corners of the store?
    2) Are the lights used to create focal points within the store?
    3) Are the lights using the correct bulbs? Are the fluorescent bulbs all cool or warm or are they a mixed bag? Are all the incandescent lights standard spots and floods or are they a more current quartz lamp?

G) Counter Area
    1) Does the counter utilize point of sale merchandising techniques?
    2) Is a showcase incorporated into the checkout counter and is it lit?
    3) Is the wall behind the checkout counter well-merchandised with impulse items?

H) Dressing Rooms
    1) Are the dressing rooms properly located to maximize traffic flow and inhibit shoplifting?
    2) Are the dressing rooms at least 42" square and do they contain a seat, mirror, a light over the mirror (not the customer) and a clothing hook?

I) Traffic Patterns
    1) Does traffic flow throughout your store?
    2) Are sales slower in one area of the store no matter what merchandise you put there?
    3) Are logical traffic patterns identifiable, or are fixtures scattered so randomly the customer has little idea how to get around the store?

J) Colors
    1) Are your colors soothing or do they clash with each other or the merchandise? Are the colors consistent with the type of merchandise you are selling?
    2) Are the color details consistent throughout the store including the flooring, ceiling, walls and fixtures, or does a combination of new, used and vendor equipment, create a kaleidoscope?
    3) What is the physical condition of the interior paint? Does the store need repainting?

K) Merchandising
    1) Is the merchandise presented in an attractive, interesting manner?
    2) Is compatible and/or complimentary merchandise displayed together or in close proximity?
    3) Have focal, high and stocking points been utilized to attract attention and encourage traffic flow?
    4) Is interior signage used effectively and are signs neatly lettered?
    5) Are enough mirrors used in the store?

L) Fixtures and equipment
    1) Are the fixtures clean and unbroken?
    2) Are the fixtures consistent or a combination of new and used equipment?
    3) Are the fixtures dated in style, color or both?
    4) Do the fixtures do what you want them to do?
    5) Do the showcases have lights and pads?

M) Cleanliness
    1) Is the store clean? Floors vacuumed, tiles waxed and buffed?
    2) Is the merchandise clean and orderly?
    3) Are the aisles clear of boxes and merchandise waiting to be set out?

N) HVAC
    1) Do the heating and air conditioning work correctly and is either currently affecting the comfort of your customers?

I encourage you to use this checklist on a regular basis and to add your own questions. Share the list with your managers and employees so they will take note of the areas that need work. In the long run, it's the merchant who pays consistent attention to detail who will succeed where others fail.

12

12 RETAIL CONSTRUCTION AND REMODELING

Building or remodeling a store is rarely an enjoyable experience. In fact, for the neophyte, construction is often nothing but misery. Everything takes longer than planned. Everything costs more than originally estimated. By the time the job is complete, you are convinced you should be a general contractor because if the person who handled your project can make that much money, you could be a millionaire in six months. Believe it or not, there are contractors who are proficient and bring jobs in on time and within budget. They are just hard to find.

I've been involved in construction as an attorney, builder, designer, supplier and project manager for 16 years and I think I've finally figured out why there are so many horror stories. It's because most construction jobs utilize so many people. The work usually requires a series of subcontractors, and in retail the respective skills and duties of the parties involved are something like this:

1) General contractor: Bids the entire job, fine-tunes the plans with the designer, obtains permits, hires the subs, choreographs the order of work performed, pays attention to detail, handles all inspections, pays subs as required, makes sure the work is completed per plan and on time, and collects most of the money.

2) The general contractor most often works with the following subs:

    a) floorcovering firm
    b) carpenter
    c) electrician
    d) sheet rock hanger and taper
    e) painter
    f) plumber
    g) ceiling installer
    h) sprinkler installer
    i) cabinet maker/fixture supplier
    j) glazer (storefront glass and interior mirrors)
    k) sign supplier
    l) heating and air conditioning contractor

3) All of these subs in turn cannot do their jobs if the manufacturer has not supplied the required parts and supplies. So, if parts are late, subs are late. Further, most subs have people on staff who are not reliable. Why? Because reliable people cost more than many subs care to part with, so the only jobs that get priority and good people are those favored by the sub due to either continuity of work (the general works with this sub all the time) or high profit.

4) On many jobs, things go wrong on a daily basis. The carpet is set to be installed on

BEACH CONSTRUCTION
CONTRACT FOR SERVICES

Date of Agreement: July 6, 1995
Owner: Joe Smith
Contractor: Beach Construction
Project: Smith Surf/ La Jolla
Contract Documents submitted by: Jay Display
Date and ID # of Contract Documents: Jan. 30, 1995

The Owner and Contractor agree as set forth below.

Article 1. The Work
The Contractor shall perform all the Work required by the contract Documents.

Article 2. Time of Commencement and Substantial Completion
The work to be commenced under this contract shall commence July 6, 1995 and subject to authorized adjustments shall be achieved not later than August 27, 1995.

If Contractor is delayed at any time in the progress of the work by changes in the work, fire, unusual delay in transportation, law (eg. permit problems), or adverse weather conditions, or any other causes beyond the Contractors control including delay in receipt of store fixtures and equipment or floorcoverings, the competition date shall be extended for a reasonable time as justified by the delay.

Article 3. Contract Sum
The contract sum for performance of the work subject to additions and deductions as authorized by the owner shall be $7937.00
Prices breakdown for work is shown on Schedule A, attached.

Article 4. Progress Payments
Payments for the work shall be made as follows: 35% of the contract amount in advance. 25% after framing and drywall, 30% after electric, balance, 10% on installation of fixtures.
In the event payments are not made as specified Contractor may cease the work until such time as payments have been made, the completion date shall be extended by a like time period.

Article 5. Facilities
The Owner shall provide adequate facilities for delivery, unloading, staging and storage in accordance with a mutually agreed upon schedule.

Article 6. Miscellaneous Provisions
6.1 The contract shall be governed by the law of the state of California.
6.2 Any claims or disputes arising out of this agreement shall be settled by arbitration in accordance with the rules of the American Arbitration Association unless the parties mutually agree otherwise.

Article 7. Insurance
Contractor and his Subs shall maintain adequate liability and workman's compensation insurance covering the work.

Article 8. Other Provisions
Owner shall be responsible for paint, plumbing, and permits.

Agreed to this date.

Owner   Contractor

_____   _____

Date _____   Date _____

Wednesday and by Tuesday still hasn't arrived from the mill in Georgia. The cabinet maker has all the rough cabinets built but the laminate manufacturer is out of stock, won't be in stock soon and no replacement color is available. The electrician got a deal on the track lighting so he substituted for what was specified and you hate the new lights. The painter got the colors reversed so the walls are now blue and the trim beige. Etc., etc. Every horror story you've ever heard is probably true, so simply get ready. Never, never, never plan an opening party in close proximity to your planned opening date. Give yourself at least two to four weeks to correct for mistakes and do some fine-tuning.

5) Given all the people involved and the caliber of the help, it is a wonder any job gets completed. How do you protect yourself?

   a) Hire a general contractor with references on similar jobs.
   b) Get several bids. Make sure the bidders are bidding on the same thing. Don't take the low bid simply because it is the lowest.
   c) Never give a contractor too much money in advance.
   d) Expect the worst and plan for it fiscally and psychologically.
   e) Track the work progress on a daily basis.
   f) Establish a firm schedule of events.
   g) Be reasonable. Do not create an adversarial relationship with your General Contractor. You need him!

Go over your contracts for work details, materials and insurance carefully. Set up progress payments based on work completed. Establish a retention amount of at least 10% to be paid 14 to 30 days after completion of the work to cover all contingencies. Let the contractor know that time is of the essence on the job and any delays will be costing you substantial income and expense. Set up penalty clauses for avoidable late completion dates. Go over all contracts with a competent attorney. Yes, it will cost an extra $500 for the lawyer. So what? You're spending thousands of dollars on the store. Cover your fanny.

ALTERNATIVES TO GENERAL CONTRACTORS

There are alternatives to using a contractor. You can do the work yourself if you have the necessary skills to do much of the carpentry, painting, electric, etc. The bigger problem is time. If you don't have an existing business to stay on top of, doing the construction work may make sense. On the other hand, if you have to take care of an operating store, it may be very difficult to find the time to participate in or supervise the construction. In fact, it may wind up being a waste of your time which is probably more profitably spent minding your primary business.

On a personal note, in 1985 I decided to build an office/showroom for my company in San Francisco. The bids I received for construction were so high I decided to take my own crew up. We built out 3000 square feet of showroom in 7 days and I saved close to $20,000. I felt justified in taking the time off from my design efforts to get a little dirty and pound a few nails.

The alternative to using a contractor or doing the work yourself is to act as a General, subbing the work to the various trades. If you have the time, this may not be a bad idea. The General normally charges 15 to 20% of the total contract cost as his profit and overhead plus a supervision fee. On a $30,000, project this can amount to about $10,000.

The downside is, of course that you may lack experience in construction so you really don't know what the heck you are doing, who does a good job and who doesn't, how to schedule, how long things take, how much things should cost, etc. You stand a good chance of being manipulated by your subs. The result, a project brought in late, over budget and ill-finished.

Think about the construction of the store early in the design phase so the expense can be factored into the budget. Finally, be realistic about your own prowess as a builder. My firm has had to salvage many a self-builder's project that floundered halfway through the construction phase. Beyond that, if your spouse is involved in your project, you will often wish you had hired a General who you could later blame for all the problems incurred.

Notes

13

13 CHOREOGRAPHY

As with any project that requires a serious investment of time and energy, care should be taken to cover all the bases in planning your store. Just as you must give your product vendors sufficient time to manufacture and ship the merchandise you plan to sell, offer the same courtesy to your store designer, contractor and fixture supplier. Plan ahead. Don't try to jump into a new store or a remodel overnight. Take the time to figure out what you want to do, when you want to do it, and how much money you have to do it with.

How do you come up with a rational approach to coordinating all the details involved? I tend to think of a store's creation as a series of interdependent steps that must be taken in the proper sequence or the whole effort can turn into chaos. Those steps go something like this:

1) Idea: The idea is formed to create a new store or to remodel your existing space.

2) Store location and size: Are you remodeling your existing space or planning a new one? In either event you will need to ascertain the size, shape and rental cost of your new store.

3) Budget: Once the space has been ascertained, establish the people and merchandise costs. It will then be possible for you to set a reasonable budget for building the store. In most cases, that budget will need to be adequate to provide for design, flooring, equipment, lighting, signage and construction.

4) Design: Armed with a location and a budget, the retailer can approach the designer with the tools necessary to plan a store, and preliminary discussions can begin regarding design and merchandising concepts. If you don't plan to use a designer, meet with a store equipment salesperson as soon as possible and try to develop a workable store plan.

If you work with a store fixture company and unless you or the salesperson has a good eye for color, get some design help on the finish specifications. This type of consulting should not take more than a few hours and will be well worth the investment.

5) Meet with the store builders: Soon after the preliminary meeting with the designer, the retailer and designer should meet with the equipment supplier, the floor-covering dealer and the general contractor to coordinate the project's rough costs. Some designers are not conversant with retail operations and even those who are may not be familiar with current equipment systems available off-the-shelf to the retail industry.

A general contractor and equipment dealer can provide input into construction and fixture costs that will impact eventual design considerations. An early meeting may save the tenant considerable design time and money. Many times I have consulted with a design or architectural firm that was out of touch with retail construction or equipment costs. They were working with the retailers' $25,000 budget but were planning a store that was going to cost $50,000.

6) Have the job bid: Just because you conferred with a contractor or equipment house does not lock you into using them. When the plans are done, have them bid. If you are comfortable with the firms you have worked with in the preliminary stages and their bids are higher than others, share the other bids with them and see if they can sharpen their pencils. Remember, price is not everything and in the long run you may pay a little more, but get more for your money.

7) Order the equipment: As soon as the plans are bid and permits procured, order your equipment and floorcoverings. Delays in these products are not infrequent and the dealers usually cannot guarantee delivery because they have no control over the factory producing the goods.

8) Follow up: Check on the progress of the construction and the availability of the equipment and flooring regularly. Don't assume that the contractor has all facets of the choreography under control. He may be so occupied with the construction that he has not adequately coordinated with the floorcovering dealer or the equipment supplier. Better that you do a little extra follow-up and avoid problems that may crop up later.

9) Don't plan to open on time: Do not plan a grand opening any sooner than 30 days from the projected opening date. Stores are rarely fully ready when they are supposed to be.

10) Merchandise properly: Give yourself time to set up the store. Nothing is worse than opening a store that looks empty or disorganized.

11) Finally, prepare for the ordeal: These projects are rarely fun no matter how experienced your help is. Things go wrong. Get ready. What is an ideal time frame for a projects developmental process from initial concept to final drawings and construction?

• Store planning and working drawings	1 to 4 weeks
• Obtaining the building permit	1 to 3 weeks
• Bidding the job (this can take place while the permit is being processed)	1 to 2 weeks
• Equipment and floorcoverings	2 to 5 weeks
• Store build-out, depending upon complexity and size	2 to 8 weeks
• Merchandising the store	2 to 8 days

The bottom line: For a 1,000 to 3,000-square-foot retail space, without extensive construction, give yourself four to eight weeks from the time you contract with a designer. For a new store in a new mall with extensive build-outs required, give yourself 6 to 12 weeks for the same job. Finally, give yourself, the designer and the contractor as much lead time in advance as possible. It will save you time, money and stress.

OTHER STORE PLANS

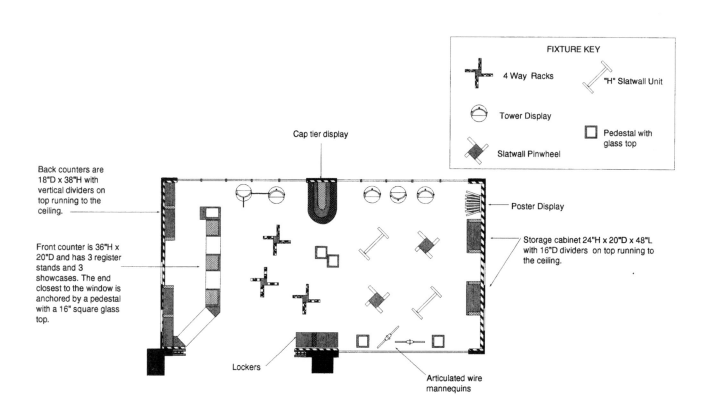

FIXTURE KEY

4 Way Racks

"H" Slatwall Unit

Tower Display

Pedestal with glass top

Slatwall Pinwheel

Cap tier display

Back counters are 18"D x 38"H with vertical dividers on top running to the ceiling.

Front counter is 36"H x 20"D and has 3 register stands and 3 showcases. The end closest to the window is anchored by a pedestal with a 16" square glass top.

Poster Display

Storage cabinet 24"H x 20"D x 48"L with 16"D dividers on top running to the ceiling.

Lockers

Articulated wire mannequins

1000 Sq. Ft. Team
Sports Shop

FIXTURE PLAN

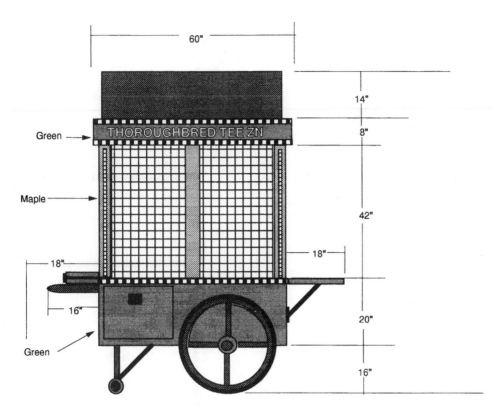

60"

14"

8"

Green → THOROUGHBRED TEE ZN

Maple →

42"

18"   18"

16"

20"

Green

16"

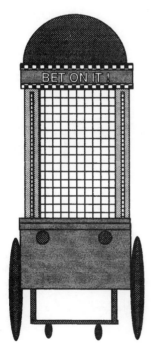

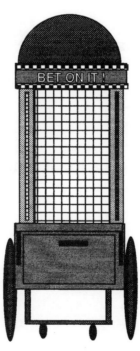

BET ON IT !   BET ON IT !

Display Cart
for Apparel and
Gift

TRIO DISPLAY
ATTN: JEFF GRANT
619.454.3134

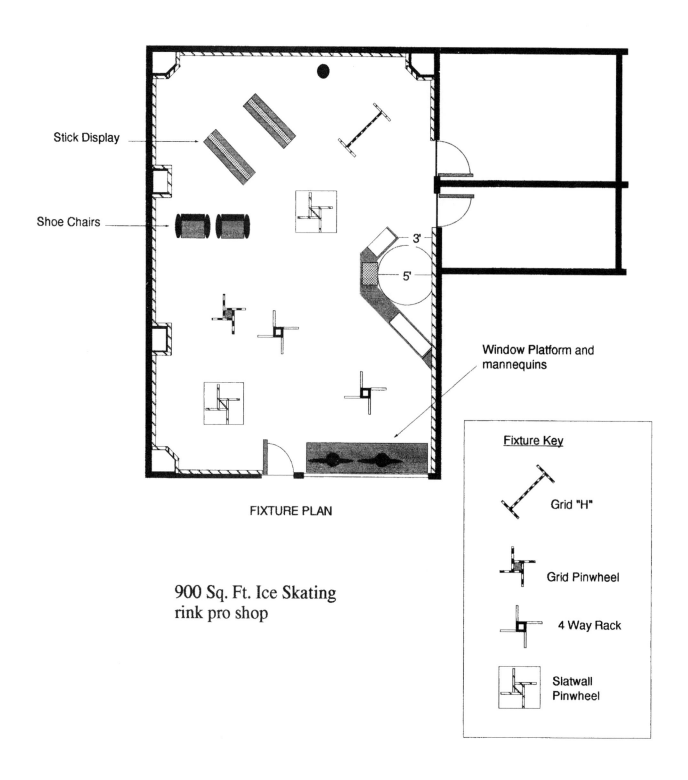

Stick Display

Shoe Chairs

3'

5'

Window Platform and mannequins

FIXTURE PLAN

Fixture Key

Grid "H"

Grid Pinwheel

4 Way Rack

Slatwall Pinwheel

900 Sq. Ft. Ice Skating rink pro shop

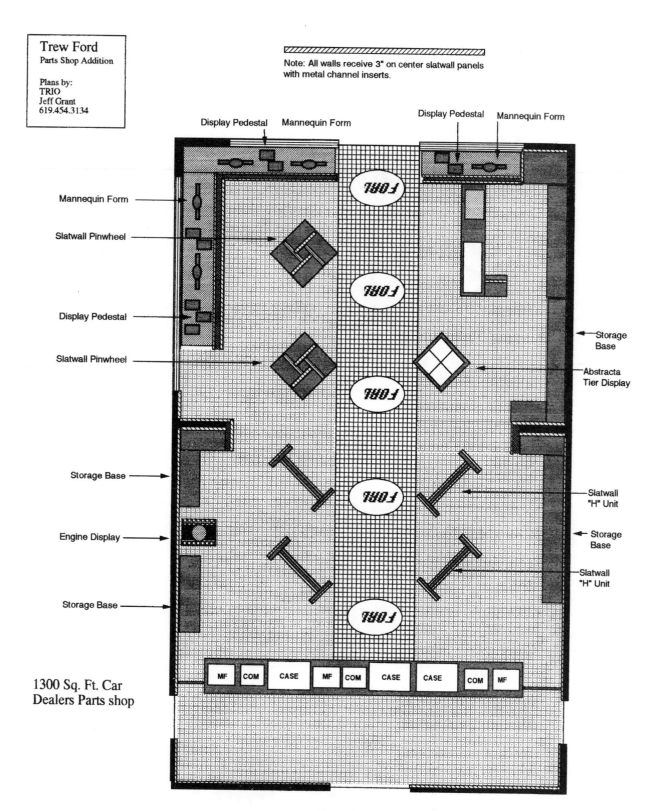

Trew Ford
Parts Shop Addition

Plans by:
TRIO
Jeff Grant
619.454.3134

Note: All walls receive 3" on center slatwall panels
with metal channel inserts.

Display Pedestal Mannequin Form

Display Pedestal Mannequin Form

Mannequin Form

Slatwall Pinwheel

Display Pedestal

Slatwall Pinwheel

Storage Base

Abstracta Tier Display

Storage Base

Slatwall "H" Unit

Engine Display

Storage Base

Slatwall "H" Unit

Storage Base

1300 Sq. Ft. Car
Dealers Parts shop

FORD
FORD
FORD
FORD
FORD

| MF | COM | CASE | MF | COM | CASE | CASE | COM | MF |

STORE FIXTURES & FITTINGS

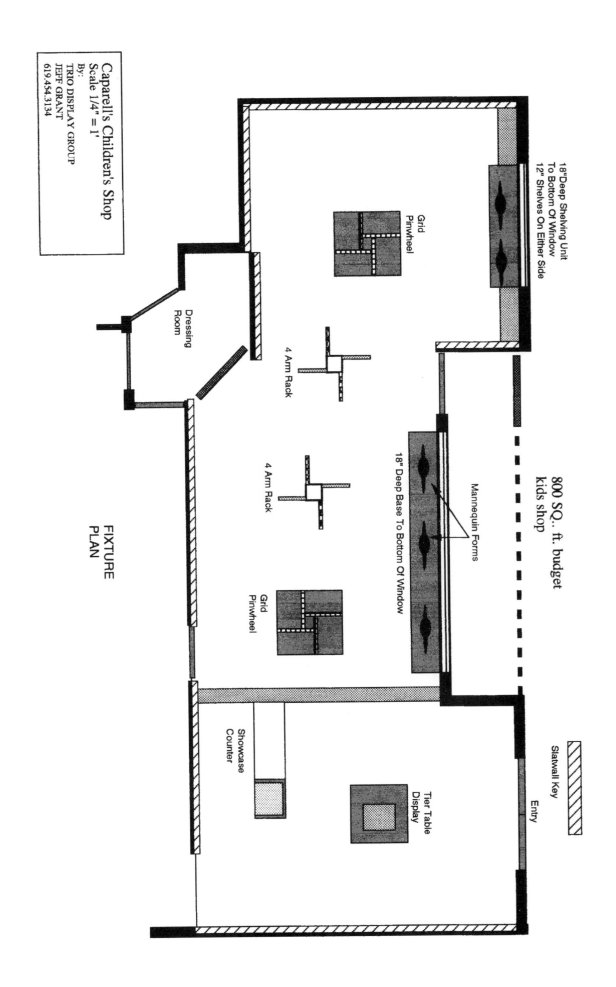

Caparell's Children's Shop
Scale 1/4" = 1'
By:
TRIO DISPLAY GROUP
JEFF GRANT
619.454.3134

FIXTURE
PLAN

Dressing
Room

4 Arm Rack

4 Arm Rack

Grid
Pinwheel

Grid
Pinwheel

18"Deep Shelving Unit
To Bottom Of Window
12" Shelves On Either Side

800 SQ.. ft. budget
kids shop

Mannequin Forms

18" Deep Base To Bottom Of Window

Slatwall Key

Entry

Showcase
Counter

Tier Table
Display

Budget museum gift shop fixture plan

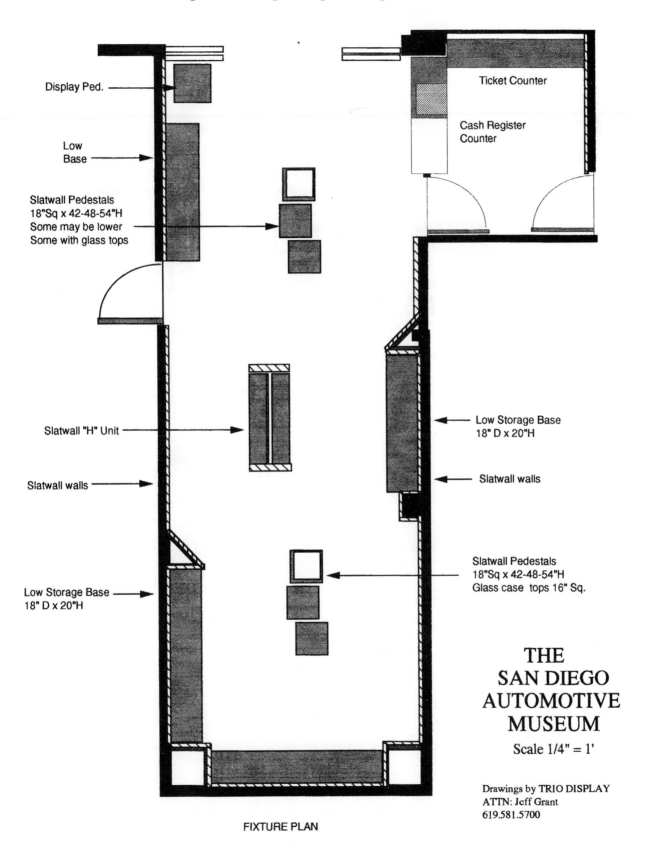

Display Ped.

Low
Base

Slatwall Pedestals
18"Sq x 42-48-54"H
Some may be lower
Some with glass tops

Slatwall "H" Unit

Slatwall walls

Low Storage Base
18" D x 20"H

Ticket Counter

Cash Register
Counter

Low Storage Base
18" D x 20"H

Slatwall walls

Slatwall Pedestals
18"Sq x 42-48-54"H
Glass case tops 16" Sq.

THE
SAN DIEGO
AUTOMOTIVE
MUSEUM

Scale 1/4" = 1'

Drawings by TRIO DISPLAY
ATTN: Jeff Grant
619.581.5700

FIXTURE PLAN

1000 Sq. ft. hospital gift shop. the budget
for this store was approx. $30,000

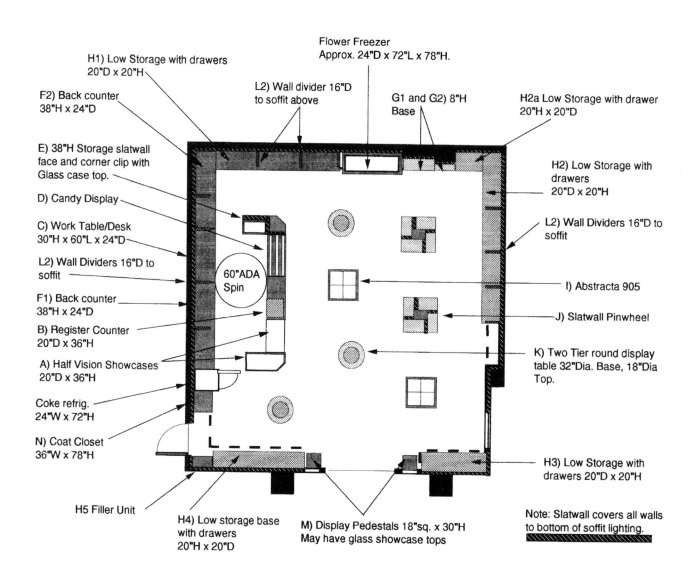

H1) Low Storage with drawers
20"D x 20"H

F2) Back counter
38"H x 24"D

E) 38"H Storage slatwall
face and corner clip with
Glass case top.

D) Candy Display

C) Work Table/Desk
30"H x 60"L x 24"D

L2) Wall Dividers 16"D to
soffit

F1) Back counter
38"H x 24"D

B) Register Counter
20"D x 36"H

A) Half Vision Showcases
20"D x 36"H

Coke refrig.
24"W x 72"H

N) Coat Closet
36"W x 78"H

H5 Filler Unit

Flower Freezer
Approx. 24"D x 72"L x 78"H.

L2) Wall divider 16"D
to soffit above

G1 and G2) 8"H
Base

H2a Low Storage with drawer
20"H x 20"D

H2) Low Storage with
drawers
20"D x 20"H

L2) Wall Dividers 16"D to
soffit

I) Abstracta 905

J) Slatwall Pinwheel

K) Two Tier round display
table 32"Dia. Base, 18"Dia
Top.

H3) Low Storage with
drawers 20"D x 20"H

60"ADA
Spin

H4) Low storage base
with drawers
20"H x 20"D

M) Display Pedestals 18"sq. x 30"H
May have glass showcase tops

Note: Slatwall covers all walls
to bottom of soffit lighting.

FIXTURE PLAN

El Camino Hospital
New Gift Shop
Scale: 1/8"= 1'
Plan Set Date 5-19-94

Drawings by
TRIO Display
Jeff Grant
619.454.3134

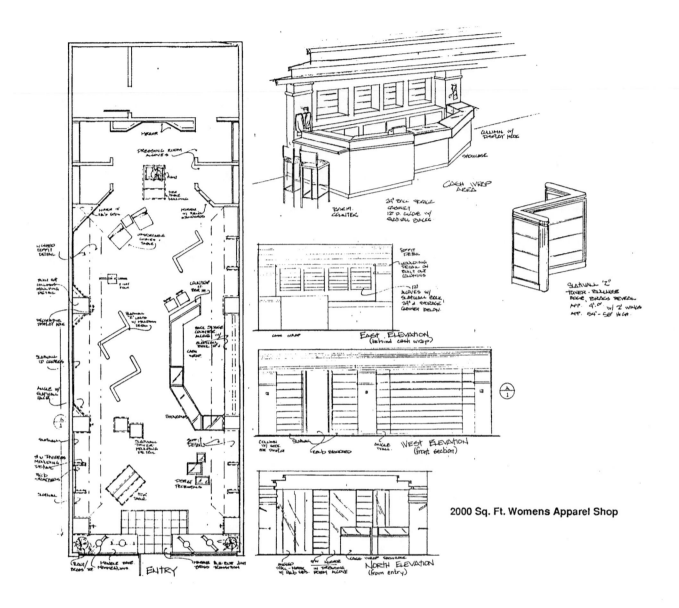

2000 Sq. Ft. Womens Apparel Shop

Glossary

Abstracta: A connector and tube system used to create fixtures, displays, and exhibits.

Beamspread: The diameter of the circle of light crated by a light bulb. Beamspreads will increase or decrease based on the type of bulb used (spot or flood), the bulb's intensity, and its distance from the object it is casting its light on.

Bins: Usually 10-inch square by 16-inches deep, glass, wire or wood bins used to stock shirts, sweats or other clothing.

Build-Ups: A series of geometric shapes used to display products at different heights. Usually made from plexiglas or wood. However, any small prop will do as long as it does not conflict with the product.

Card Holder: A plex or metal holder used to display informational signs within the store. Available in many sizes and for both floor and counter signage.

Carded: Term for merchandise that is delivered to the retailer attached to a display cards, like jewelry, small toys, etc. Usually displayed on peg hooks or special plastic fixtures.

Cash-wrap: The front counter/check-out area of a store that houses the cash register and wrapping section.

Chain Stores: A group of stores that are centrally owned and managed.

Diffuser: A shield that softens the glare from a light fixture.

Dump Tables: A rimmed table placed on the sales floor that is used to feature sale or special merchandise. Heavily used in discount operations.

Elevations: A drawing of the store shown as if the walls had been stood up and viewed from inside the store. In a standard store plan, elevations are usually shown of all wall surfaces.

Face Out: Displaying clothing front-forward rather than side-hung.

Floor Plan: An architectural drawing showing the length and width of a store and the location of the fixtures and displays.

Forms: Display element used to merchandise items of clothing. Forms may be flat or fully contoured, but they are distinguishable from mannequins in that they don't have full body parts. A form might be just a bust or just a pair of legs.

Four Way Rack: A four-armed presentation rack used to display clothing at multiple levels.

Gondola: A display fixture usually configured as an "H" with a 48-inch-wide by 54-inch-high center panel and 36-inch-wide by 54-inch-high end panels. A base anchors the unit and shelves or hangbars are used on all sides for merchandise presentation.

HVAC: Construction vernacular for heating, ventilating and air conditioning.

Keystone: A product that costs a merchant $1.00 is sold for $2.00. This doubling of the cost of goods to arrive at a sales price is called "keystoning."

Mannequin: A three-dimensional figure used to display clothing. Mannequins may be very realistic or completely abstract. Available in many sizes and finishes and as men, women, kids, teens, etc.

Outriggers: Wood or metal uprights, usually 7 to 8 feet high with slotted standard backs. Used to support shelves or hangbar along a wall.

Rendering: A life-like perspective drawing of a store.

Round Rack: A 36 or 42-inch diameter round rack used to display clothing. Holds many more pieces of apparel than a presentation rack (2 or 4 arm).

Shrinkage: Theft or a store's merchandise.

Shopdrawings: A working drawing that a shop or contractor can use to actually build from.

Shopfitter: A European term for those professionals who work with a merchant to provide a turn-key store. Shopfitters provide design, construction, and equipment services all under one roof.

Slatwall: A 4 by 8-foot panel of wood with or without plastic laminate face. The panel is routed with slots that will accept display equipment and is mounted to the wall in a store for merchandising product.

Soffit: An overhead component of a building such as a dropped ceiling, an arch, a beam or a cornice.

Standards: Vertical channels of metal which are slotted to accept display brackets and are attached to walls for merchandising product.

Tempered Glass: Safety glass that has been manufactured in such a way that it shatters into small pieces rather than dangerous shards when it breaks.

Vendor: The person or company from whom the retailer buys his products.

Waterfall: An arm that attaches to a rack or a wall and is used to present merchandise front forward.

Notes

Notes

Notes

Notes

Notes

Notes

Notes